Generative AI

A Comprehensive Guide

Copyright © 2024. All rights reserved.

No part of this book may be reproduced, stored in a retrieval system, or transmitted in any form or by any means without prior written permission from the publisher, except for brief quotations used in reviews or scholarly work.

ISBN: 9798339824312

Table of Contents

Abstract 1

Part I: Introduction to Generative AI 2

Chapter 01: Generative AI 3

Introduction 3

Overview of Generative AI 3

Key Characteristics of Generative AI 4

Historical Context and Evolution 4

Importance and Impact on Various Industries 7

Creative Industries: 7

Healthcare: 8

Gaming and Virtual Reality: 9

Finance: 9

Manufacturing and Supply Chain: 10

Challenges and Ethical Considerations 11

Bias in AI Models: 11

Ethical Use of Generated Content: 11

Security Concerns: 12

Environmental Impact: 13

Future Prospects and Trends in Generative AI 13

Advancements in Model Architectures: 13

Ethical and Responsible AI Development: 14

Integration with Human Creativity: 14

New Applications and Use Cases: 15

Summary 15

Key Takeaways 16

Chapter 02: Key Concepts and Terminologies 17

Introduction 17

Deep Learning and Neural Networks 17

Supervised vs. Unsupervised Learning... 18

Generative Models: An Overview 20

Types of Generative Models: 20

Common Algorithms in Generative AI... 21

Summary... 24

Key Takeaways 25

Part II: Generative Models and Techniques 27

Chapter 03: Generative Adversarial Networks (GANs).. 28

Introduction 28

Introduction to GANs.. 28

Foundational Concept 28

Adversarial Setup... 29

Impact and Significance... 29

How GANs Work: The Generator and Discriminator 29

The Generator: 29

The Discriminator:... 30

Training Process: 30

Types of GANs.. 31

Deep Convolutional GAN (DCGAN): 31

StyleGAN:... 32

CycleGAN:.. 32

Applications of GANs 33

Summary 34

Key Takeaways 35

Chapter 04: Variational Autoencoders (VAEs) 37

Introduction 37

Introduction to VAEs 37

Historical Context and Development 37

Architectural Components: 38

Training Process: 38

Latent Space Representation 39

Encoding Data: 39

Sampling from Latent Space: 39

Regularization and Structure: 40

Applications of VAEs in Image and Data Generation 40

Image Generation: 40

Data Augmentation: 41

Text and Speech Generation: 41

Anomaly Detection: 41

Data Compression and Denoising: 42

Summary 42

Key Takeaways 42

Chapter 05: Transformer Models 44

Introduction 44

Introduction to Transformers 44

Architectural Overview 45

Encoder-Decoder Structure 45

Layers 45

Positional Encoding 45

Advantages: 45

Attention Mechanism 45

Self-Attention: 46

Scaled Dot-Product Attention 46

Multi-Head Attention 46

Cross-Attention: 46

GPT (Generative Pre-trained Transformers) and its Variants ... 47

BERT and Other Transformer-Based Models 49

Summary 52

Key Takeaways 52

Chapter 06: Diffusion Models 53

Introduction 53

Introduction to Diffusion Models 53

Conceptual Foundation: 53

Mathematical Formulation: 54

Training Dynamics: 54

How Diffusion Processes Generate Data 55

Forward Diffusion Process: 55

Reverse Denoising Process: 55

Advanced Techniques: 55

Applications in Image and Audio Generation 56

Image Generation 56

Audio Generation 57

Summary 57

Key Takeaways 58

Part III: Applications of Generative AI 59

Chapter 07: Text Generation 60

Introduction 60

Language Models: GPT, BERT, T5 60

GPT (Generative Pre-trained Transformer) 60

BERT (Bidirectional Encoder Representations from Transformers) 61

T5 (Text-to-Text Transfer Transformer) 62

Natural Language Processing (NLP) Applications 63

Text Generation 63

Text Summarization 64

Machine Translation 64

Sentiment Analysis 65

Chatbots and Conversational AI 65

Functionality 65

Applications 66

Challenges 66

Ethical Considerations in Text Generation 67

Misinformation and Fake News 67

Bias and Fairness 67

Privacy and Security 68

Accountability and Transparency 68

Summary 69

Key Takeaways 69

Chapter 08: Image Generation 70

Introduction 70

Tools and Techniques: DALL-E, CLIP, StyleGAN 70

DALL-E 70

CLIP (Contrastive Language-Image Pretraining) 71

StyleGAN 72
Creating Art, Logos, and Visual Content 73
Art Creation 73
Logo Design 73
Visual Content for Marketing 74
Deepfakes: Creation and Detection 74
Creation of Deepfakes 74
Detection of Deepfakes 75
Legal and Ethical Issues in Image Generation 75
Copyright and Intellectual Property 76
Misuse and Harmful Content 76
Ethical Considerations 77
Summary 77
Key Takeaways 77

Chapter 09: Music and Audio Generation 79

Introduction 79
AI in Music Composition 79
Generative Models for Music 79
Interactive Composition Tools 80
Music Style Transfer 81
Tools and Models for Audio Generation 81
Music Generation Tools 81
Audio Generation Models 82
Speech Synthesis and Voice Generation 82
Applications in Film, Games, and Media 83
Film and Television 83
Video Games 83

Media and Advertising 84
Summary 84
Key Takeaways 85

Chapter 10: Video and Animation Generation 86

Introduction 86
Video Synthesis Techniques 86
Generative Adversarial Networks (GANs) 86
Variational Autoencoders (VAEs) 87
Reinforcement Learning (RL) 88
Neural Rendering 88
Applications in Film, Animation, and Virtual Reality 89
Film Production 89
Animation 89
Virtual Reality (VR) 90
Challenges and Future Directions 90
Challenges 90
Future Directions 91
Summary 92
Key Takeaways 92

Chapter 11: Generative AI in Healthcare 93

Introduction 93
Drug Discovery and Development 93
1. Accelerating Drug Discovery 93
2. Enhancing Drug Repurposing 94
3. Optimizing Clinical Trials 94
Medical Imaging and Diagnostics 95
1. Image Enhancement 95

2. Automated Image Analysis 95
3. Enhancing Diagnostic Accuracy 96
Personalized Treatment Plans 96
1. Genomic Data Analysis 96
2. Optimizing Treatment Regimens 97
Key Takeaways 98

Part IV: Advanced Topics in Generative AI 99

Chapter 12: Ethical and Social Implications 100

Introduction 100
AI Bias and Fairness 100
1. Sources of AI Bias 100
2. Addressing AI Bias 101
Ownership and Intellectual Property 102
1. Ownership of AI-Generated Content 102
2. Ethical Implications of AI-Generated Content 103
The Role of AI in Society: Risks and Rewards 103
1. Risks Associated with AI 104
2. Rewards and Opportunities 104
Summary 105
Key Takeaways 106

Chapter 13: Challenges in Generative AI 107

Introduction 107
Quality Control and Content Coherence 107
Content Accuracy and Reliability 107
Consistency and Relevance 108
Evaluation Metrics and Methods 108
Computational Requirements 109

Hardware and Infrastructure 109
Resource Efficiency and Optimization 109
Cost Management 109
Managing and Mitigating Ethical Concerns 110
Preventing Misuse 110
Addressing Bias and Fairness 110
Transparency and Accountability 111
Privacy and Data Security 111
Societal and Long-Term Implications 112
Impact on Employment and Labor Markets 112
Social and Cultural Impact 112
Future Research and Development 112
Summary 113
Key Takeaways 113

Chapter 14: Integrating Generative AI with Other Technologies 115

Introduction 115
AI and IoT: Smart Content Creation 115
Enhancing IoT Devices with Generative AI 115
Personalized User Experiences 116
Integration Challenges and Solutions 116
AI in Cloud Computing 117
Scalability and Resource Management 117
Collaborative Development and Deployment 117
Enhanced AI Services and Tools 117
Cross-Disciplinary Applications and Innovations 118
Integrating AI with Healthcare Technologies 118

Enhancing Creative Industries 118

Advancing Scientific Research 118

Future Directions and Innovations 119

Emerging Technologies and AI Integration 119

Interdisciplinary Research and Development 119

Summary 120

Key Takeaways 120

Part V: The Future of Generative AI 122

Chapter 15: Emerging Trends in Generative AI 123

Introduction 123

AI and Augmented Creativity 123

Expanding Creative Horizons 123

Innovative Creative Tools 124

Interactive Art and Performance 124

Personalized Content Generation 125

Tailoring Digital Experiences 125

Adaptive Learning and Personalization 125

Enhancing User Engagement 125

Generative AI in the Metaverse 126

Crafting Immersive Virtual Worlds 126

Realistic Avatars and NPCs 126

Enhancing Metaverse Experiences 127

Future Directions and Innovations 127

Advancements in AI Creativity Tools 127

Integration with Emerging Technologies 127

Cross-Disciplinary Collaborations 128

AI and Human Collaboration 128

AI in Business and Industry 128
Summary 129
Key Takeaways 129

Chapter 16: The Road Ahead 130

Introduction 130
Future Research Directions 130
Advancements in Model Architectures 130
Enhancing Data Efficiency 131
Ethical and Responsible AI 131
Potential Breakthroughs and Innovations 132
Advanced Generative Models 132
AI for Complex Problem Solving 132
Enhanced Human-AI Collaboration 133
Generative AI's Role in Shaping the Future 133
Transforming Industries 133
Redefining Human Experience 134
Addressing Global Challenges 134
Summary 135
Key Takeaways 135

Part VI: Applications and Case Studies 136

Chapter 17: Hands-On Projects 137

Introduction 137
Building a Simple GAN from Scratch 137
Overview 137
Project Setup 137
Key Considerations 140
Implementing a Text Generator Using GPT 141

Overview 141

Project Setup 141

Key Considerations 143

Creating Art with StyleGAN 143

Overview 143

Project Setup 143

Key Considerations 144

Summary 145

Key Takeaways 145

Chapter 18: Generative AI in Computer Vision 146

Introduction 146

Image Synthesis and Enhancement: Creating and Refining Visual Content 146

Image Synthesis: Generating Realistic and Novel Visuals 146

Image Enhancement: Improving Image Quality and Clarity 147

DeepFakes: Creation and Detection in the Digital Age 147

Creation of DeepFakes: Manipulating Media with AI 147

Detection of DeepFakes: Safeguarding Truth in Media 148

Super-Resolution Imaging: Elevating Image Detail and Quality 148

Techniques in Super-Resolution: From Blurry to Clear 148

Applications in Industry: Broadening the Impact 149

Style Transfer and Artistic Creation: Merging Art and Technology 149

Style Transfer: Blending Artistic Styles with Reality 149

Artistic Creation: AI as a Creative Partner 150

3D Model Generation: Building the Future in Three Dimensions 150

Generative Models for 3D: From Pixels to Polygons 150

Applications in Industry: Transforming Design and Manufacturing 151

Summary 151

Key Takeaways 152

Chapter 19: Generative AI in Natural Language Processing 154

Introduction 154

Text Generation and Summarization 154

Text Generation 154

Text Summarization 155

Conversational Agents and Chatbots 156

Conversational Agents 156

Chatbots 156

Machine Translation 157

Neural Machine Translation (NMT) 157

Content Creation and Copywriting 158

Content Creation 158

Copywriting 158

Sentiment and Emotion Analysis 159

Sentiment Analysis 159

Emotion Analysis 159

Summary 160

Key Takeaways 160

Chapter 20: Generative AI in Art and Creativity 162

Introduction 162

AI-Generated Music and Art 162

AI-Generated Music 162
AI-Generated Art 163
AI in Film and Animation 164
Film 164
Animation 164
Generative Design in Architecture and Fashion 165
Architecture 165
Fashion 165
The Role of AI in Creative Writing 166
Creative Writing 166
Case Studies: AI Collaborations with Artists 167
Case Study 1: Refik Anadol 167
Case Study 2: Obvious Art Collective 167
Case Study 3: AI in Music Collaboration 167
Summary 167
Key Takeaways 168

Chapter 21: Case Studies 169
Introduction 169
Real-World Applications of Generative AI 169
Art and Entertainment 169
Healthcare 170
Text Generation and NLP 171
Image and Video Synthesis 172
Industry-Specific Implementations 172
Finance 172
Education 173
Retail 174

Lessons Learned from Successful Projects 174

Data Quality and Diversity 174

Ethical Considerations 175

Continuous Improvement 175

Summary 176

Key Takeaways 176

Part VII: Framework, Platform, and Tools 177

Chapter 22: Tools and Platforms for Generative AI . 178

Introduction 178

Overview of Popular Generative AI Frameworks 178

TensorFlow 178

PyTorch 179

Keras 180

Hugging Face Transformers 180

Platforms for Training and Deploying Models 181

Google Cloud AI Platform 181

AWS SageMaker 181

Microsoft Azure Machine Learning 182

Comparative Analysis of Tools and Libraries 183

Overview of Popular Tools (e.g., TensorFlow, PyTorch, JAX) .. 183

Specialized Libraries for GANs, VAEs, and Transformers 184

Using Pre-trained Models and Transfer Learning 185

Building and Training Your Generative AI Models 186

Deploying Generative AI Solutions 187

Summary 188

Key Takeaways 189

Chapter 23: Competitors of Generative AI 190

Introduction 190
Overview of Competitors 190
Traditional Machine Learning Models 190
Reinforcement Learning (RL) 192
Symbolic AI and Expert Systems 194
Rule-Based Systems 195
Hybrid AI Approaches 196
Human-in-the-Loop Systems 198
Emerging Technologies 199
Other Notable Technologies 200
Comparative Analysis 200
Use Cases and Applications 200
Strengths and Limitations 201
Choosing the Right Technology 201

Appendixes 203
1 - Acronyms 203
2 – Frequently Asked Questions (FAQs) 207
Chapter 01 207
Chapter 02 208
Chapter 03 210
Chapter 04 212
Chapter 05 214
Chapter 06 217
Chapter 07 219
Chapter 08 221
Chapter 09 223

A Comprehensive Guide

Chapter 10 225

Chapter 11 227

Chapter 12 228

Chapter 13 230

Chapter s14 232

Chapter 15 234

Chapter 16 236

Chapter 17 238

Chapter 18 240

Chapter 19 242

Chapter 20 243

Chapter 21 245

Chapter 22 247

Chapter 23 250

Abstract

Generative AI has emerged as a transformative force in the realm of artificial intelligence, influencing a wide array of industries and applications. This book provides a comprehensive exploration of Generative AI, unraveling its principles, techniques, and implications. It begins with an overview of Generative AI, tracing its historical evolution and emphasizing its profound impact on sectors such as creative industries, healthcare, gaming, finance, and manufacturing.

Key concepts in Generative AI, including deep learning, neural networks, and various generative models such as Generative Adversarial Networks (GANs), Variational Autoencoders (VAEs), and Transformer Models, are thoroughly examined. The book delves into the mechanisms of these models, their applications in generating text, images, audio, and video, and their role in enhancing creative and professional domains.

The discussion extends to the challenges and ethical considerations associated with Generative AI, including bias in models, the ethical use of generated content, security concerns, and the environmental impact of AI technologies. It also addresses future prospects and trends, such as advancements in model architectures, responsible AI development, and the integration of Generative AI with human creativity.

Practical applications and case studies illustrate the real-world impact of Generative AI, while advanced topics explore its role in various fields and its integration with other technologies. This book serves as a vital resource for understanding the complexities of Generative AI, it's potential to reshape industries and the ongoing developments that promise to drive the future of this dynamic field.

Part I: Introduction to Generative AI

Chapter 01: Generative AI

Introduction

Generative AI represents one of the most exciting and transformative advancements in artificial intelligence today. Unlike traditional AI, which focuses on processing and analyzing data to make decisions, generative AI goes a step further by creating new, original content that mimics the intricacies of human creativity. This capability is not only reshaping industries but also redefining the boundaries of what machines can do. As AI continues to evolve, generative AI stands at the forefront of innovation, offering unprecedented opportunities for creativity, problem-solving, and automation. In this chapter, we will explore the fundamental concepts of generative AI, trace its historical evolution, and examine its growing impact across various industries.

Overview of Generative AI

Generative AI is a rapidly advancing field within artificial intelligence (AI) focused on the creation of new and original content. Unlike traditional AI systems that are primarily concerned with analysis, classification, or decision-making based on existing data, generative AI models are designed to generate novel outputs. These outputs can range from text, images, and music to entire virtual environments, thereby enabling machines to mimic human creativity.

At the heart of generative AI is the concept of learning patterns from large datasets and using these patterns to produce content that not only resembles the training data but can also introduce variations and innovations. For example, a generative AI model trained on thousands of paintings can create new artwork that follows the stylistic patterns of the training data but is entirely unique. Similarly, a model trained on a vast corpus of text can generate coherent and contextually relevant paragraphs of text, as seen with models like GPT-3.

Key Characteristics of Generative AI

- **Creativity:** Generative AI can produce outputs that are creative and often indistinguishable from those created by humans. This creativity extends beyond simple reproduction of existing patterns, as these models can innovate by combining elements in novel ways.
- **Generalization:** While traditional AI excels at specific tasks, generative AI models are often more generalized, capable of performing a wide range of tasks from generating images and videos to writing code or composing music.
- **Interactivity:** Generative AI models can be interactive, allowing users to guide the generation process. For example, in text generation, users can provide prompts that the model then expands upon, creating a collaborative creation process.
- **Scalability:** These models can be scaled to generate content at a high volume, making them valuable in industries that require large amounts of creative output, such as advertising, entertainment, and content creation.

Generative AI's ability to create content autonomously opens up new avenues in various domains, from automating routine tasks to enhancing human creativity in unprecedented ways.

Historical Context and Evolution

The evolution of generative AI is a story of continuous innovation, marked by several key milestones in the broader field of artificial intelligence. Understanding the historical context of generative AI provides insights into its current capabilities and future potential.

The Early Days of AI (1950s-1980s):

1. Rule-Based Systems: The early AI systems were heavily reliant on rule-based approaches, where human programmers defined explicit rules for the machine to follow. These systems, while useful in specific contexts like chess or simple problem-solving, lacked the ability to generate new content or adapt to unforeseen scenarios.

2. Symbolic AI: Symbolic AI, which dominated early AI research, involved the manipulation of symbols and logical rules. These systems were powerful in structured environments but were unable to deal with the complexity and variability of real-world data.

Introduction of Neural Networks (1980s-1990s):

1. Perceptron and Multi-Layer Perceptron: The introduction of neural networks, particularly the perceptron model, represented a shift from rule-based systems to learning-based approaches. The multi-layer perceptron (MLP), with its ability to model more complex functions, laid the groundwork for modern deep learning.

2. Backpropagation: The development of backpropagation, a method for training neural networks, enabled more sophisticated learning and set the stage for the deep learning revolution.

The Deep Learning Era (2000s):

1. Convolutional Neural Networks (CNNs): CNNs became the standard for image recognition tasks, leading to breakthroughs in computer vision. These networks, with their ability to learn hierarchical features, were a precursor to generative models in visual domains.

2. Recurrent Neural Networks (RNNs): RNNs, designed for sequential data, became crucial in tasks like language modeling and speech recognition. Their ability to handle temporal dependencies paved the way for generative models in text and audio.

The Emergence of GANs (2014):

1. Generative Adversarial Networks (GANs): The invention of GANs by Ian Goodfellow introduced a novel approach to generative modeling. GANs consist of two networks—a generator and a discriminator—competing against each other. The generator creates data, while the discriminator evaluates it against real data. This adversarial process results in highly realistic outputs, revolutionizing fields like image synthesis, video generation, and even fashion design.

2. Applications and Advancements: GANs quickly found applications in various industries, from generating realistic faces and artwork to advancing medical imaging and synthetic data generation. The concept of "deepfakes," where GANs are used to create hyper-realistic fake videos, also emerged during this period, raising ethical concerns about the technology.

The Rise of Transformer Models (2018-Present):

1. Transformers and Self-Attention: The introduction of the Transformer architecture, particularly its self-attention mechanism, transformed natural language processing (NLP). Unlike previous models that relied on sequential processing, Transformers could process entire sequences of data simultaneously, leading to more efficient and effective learning.

2. GPT Models: OpenAI's GPT series, particularly GPT-3, showcased the power of Transformer models in generating human-like text. These models, trained on vast amounts of data, demonstrated an ability to generate coherent and contextually appropriate text across a wide range of topics. GPT-3's versatility and depth marked a significant milestone in generative AI, making it a tool for content creation, coding, customer service, and more.

Diffusion Models (2020s):

1. New Approaches to Generation: Diffusion models, which operate by gradually adding and then removing noise to generate data, have emerged as another powerful generative technique. These models are particularly effective in generating high-quality images, with applications in creative arts and media production.

2. Integration with Other AI Techniques: The combination of diffusion models with other AI techniques, such as GANs and Transformers, is leading to increasingly sophisticated generative systems capable of producing complex and innovative outputs.

Importance and Impact on Various Industries

Generative AI is not just a technological curiosity; it is a transformative force that is reshaping industries and redefining the boundaries of what machines can do. Its impact spans across various sectors, influencing how businesses operate, how creativity is expressed, and how innovation is driven.

Creative Industries:

1. Art and Design: Generative AI is becoming an indispensable tool for artists and designers, enabling the creation of unique visual experiences. Programs like DALL-E and StyleGAN allow users to generate images based on text prompts or merge different artistic styles. This technology is used in creating digital art, advertising visuals, and even in designing products such as fashion items and home decor. The ability of generative AI to produce high-quality, original content quickly and efficiently has opened up new avenues for creativity, allowing artists to explore ideas that would be time-consuming or impossible to achieve manually.

2. Music and Audio Production: In the music industry, generative AI is being used to compose music, generate soundtracks, and even produce entire albums. AI-driven music generators can create compositions in a variety of styles, from classical to electronic, offering musicians and producers new tools for inspiration and production. Moreover, generative AI is being used to enhance audio quality, create realistic sound effects, and even generate voiceovers for media content, making it a versatile tool in the audio production process.

3. Writing and Content Creation: Generative AI models like GPT-3 have revolutionized the field of content creation. These models can generate articles, blog posts, social media content, and even entire books. For writers, this means access to tools that can assist in brainstorming ideas, drafting content, and even performing edits. In journalism, AI-generated content is being used to produce news articles and reports quickly, especially for data-driven topics like financial markets and sports. Content creators across industries are leveraging generative AI to maintain high output levels while ensuring content quality and relevance.

Healthcare:

1. Drug Discovery and Development: Generative AI is revolutionizing drug discovery by enabling the rapid generation and testing of molecular structures. AI models can simulate chemical reactions and predict the efficacy of new compounds, significantly reducing the time and cost associated with traditional drug development processes. This technology is particularly impactful in areas such as oncology, where researchers are using generative AI to design new cancer treatments with improved targeting and reduced side effects.

2. Medical Imaging and Diagnostics: In medical imaging, generative AI is enhancing the resolution and clarity of images, enabling more accurate diagnoses. AI models can generate synthetic medical images to augment training datasets, improving the performance of diagnostic algorithms. Additionally, generative AI is being used to create 3D models of organs and tissues for surgical planning, providing doctors with detailed visualizations that aid in complex procedures.

3. Personalized Medicine: Generative AI is also contributing to the development of personalized medicine by generating models that predict individual responses to treatments. By analyzing genetic data and other patient-specific information, AI can help doctors tailor treatments to individual needs, improving outcomes and reducing the risk of adverse reactions.

Gaming and Virtual Reality:

1. Procedural Content Generation: In the gaming industry, generative AI is used to create vast and immersive worlds. AI can generate landscapes, levels, and entire environments dynamically, providing players with unique experiences each time they play. This technology is also used to create characters, quests, and storylines, making games more engaging and personalized. Procedural content generation reduces the need for manual content creation, allowing developers to focus on refining gameplay mechanics and other aspects of game design.

2. AI-Driven Characters and NPCs: Generative AI enables the creation of more realistic and interactive non-player characters (NPCs) in video games. These AI-driven characters can adapt their behavior based on player actions, providing more dynamic and unpredictable interactions. This leads to richer, more immersive gaming experiences, where players feel truly engaged with the virtual world.

3. Virtual Reality Experiences: In virtual reality (VR), generative AI is used to create realistic environments and interactive experiences. AI can generate textures, lighting, and physics in real-time, making VR experiences more immersive and believable. This technology is particularly important in VR applications for training, education, and therapy, where realistic simulations are critical for effective outcomes.

Finance:

1. Algorithmic Trading: Generative AI plays a key role in algorithmic trading by generating trading strategies based on historical market data. These models can simulate market conditions, test various scenarios, and optimize trading algorithms to maximize returns. AI-driven trading systems are capable of analyzing vast amounts of data in real-time, making rapid decisions that human traders cannot match, leading to more efficient and profitable trading operations.

2. Fraud Detection: In the financial sector, generative AI is used to detect fraudulent activities by generating models that identify unusual patterns in transactions. These models can adapt to new types of fraud, providing financial institutions with robust tools to protect their customers and assets. AI-driven fraud detection systems are particularly effective in identifying complex schemes that traditional methods might miss, such as money laundering and insider trading.

3. Risk Management: Generative AI is also transforming risk management by simulating various financial scenarios and generating models that predict potential risks. This allows institutions to develop more accurate risk assessments and create strategies to mitigate potential losses. AI-driven risk management tools are particularly valuable in areas such as credit risk assessment, where they can analyze large datasets to identify factors that may indicate a higher likelihood of default.

Manufacturing and Supply Chain:

1. Design and Prototyping: Generative AI is used in manufacturing to create optimized designs and prototypes. AI models can generate multiple design variations based on specific criteria, such as material usage, strength, and cost, allowing engineers to select the best option. This technology speeds up the design process and reduces the time and cost of prototyping, enabling manufacturers to bring products to market faster.

2. Predictive Maintenance: In supply chain management, generative AI models are used to predict equipment failures and optimize maintenance schedules. By analyzing sensor data and historical performance records, AI can generate predictions about when machines are likely to fail, allowing companies to perform maintenance before breakdowns occur. This reduces downtime, extends equipment life, and lowers maintenance costs, improving overall operational efficiency.

3. Supply Chain Optimization: Generative AI is also applied to optimize supply chain operations by generating models that predict demand, optimize inventory levels, and streamline logistics. These models can simulate various supply chain scenarios, allowing companies to make informed decisions that reduce costs and improve service levels. AI-driven supply chain optimization is particularly important in industries with complex global supply chains, where small inefficiencies can have significant impacts on profitability.

Challenges and Ethical Considerations

While generative AI holds immense potential, it also presents significant challenges and ethical considerations that need to be addressed to ensure responsible and beneficial use of the technology.

Bias in AI Models:

1. Training Data Bias: One of the major challenges in generative AI is bias in training data. Since AI models learn from existing data, any biases present in the data are likely to be reflected in the generated outputs. For example, if a generative AI model is trained on biased text or images, it may produce outputs that reinforce harmful stereotypes or exclude certain groups. This issue is particularly concerning in applications such as hiring algorithms, content generation, and predictive policing, where biased AI models can perpetuate discrimination and inequality.

2. Mitigating Bias: To address bias, it is essential to ensure that training datasets are diverse and representative of different perspectives. Additionally, developers can implement techniques such as bias detection and correction algorithms, fairness constraints, and model auditing to reduce the impact of bias on AI outputs. Ongoing research in explainable AI and fairness in machine learning is critical to developing more transparent and equitable generative AI systems.

Ethical Use of Generated Content:

1. Deepfakes and Misinformation: Generative AI has been used to create deepfakes, which are hyper-realistic videos or images that depict events or people in ways that did not actually occur. While deepfakes can be used for entertainment or educational purposes, they also have the potential to spread misinformation and manipulate public opinion. The use of deepfakes in political campaigns, for example, poses a significant threat to the integrity of democratic processes.

2. Content Ownership and Copyright: Another ethical consideration is the ownership and copyright of AI-generated content. Since AI models generate content based on existing data, questions arise about who owns the rights to the generated content and whether it infringes on the intellectual property of the original creators. Legal frameworks are still evolving in this area, and it is important for developers, users, and policymakers to engage in discussions about the fair use and attribution of AI-generated content.

3. Ensuring Accountability: To ensure ethical use of generative AI, it is important to establish clear guidelines and accountability measures for the deployment and use of AI-generated content. This may involve the implementation of watermarking technologies to identify AI-generated content, the development of ethical AI standards, and the establishment of regulatory bodies to oversee the use of generative AI in sensitive areas.

Security Concerns:

1. Adversarial Attacks: Generative AI models are vulnerable to adversarial attacks, where malicious actors manipulate the input data to deceive the AI into generating incorrect or harmful outputs. For example, an attacker could subtly alter an image to trick an AI model into generating a completely different image, leading to potential security breaches in systems that rely on AI-generated content. Adversarial attacks pose a significant risk in areas such as autonomous vehicles, where AI-generated decisions can have life-or-death consequences.

2. Data Privacy: Generative AI models often require large amounts of data for training, raising concerns about data privacy and security. The use of personal data in training AI models can lead to the generation of outputs that inadvertently reveal sensitive information. It is essential to implement robust data privacy measures, such as differential privacy techniques, to protect individuals' data while still enabling the effective use of generative AI.

Environmental Impact:

1. Energy Consumption: Training large generative AI models requires significant computational resources, leading to high energy consumption and a substantial carbon footprint. As the demand for AI-generated content increases, so does the environmental impact of training and deploying these models. This issue is particularly pressing in the context of climate change, where reducing energy consumption is a global priority.

2. Sustainable AI Practices: To mitigate the environmental impact of generative AI, it is important to develop and adopt sustainable AI practices. This may include optimizing model architectures for efficiency, using renewable energy sources for data centers, and exploring alternative approaches to AI training that reduce energy consumption. Additionally, researchers and developers can focus on creating smaller, more efficient models that achieve similar performance with lower computational costs.

Future Prospects and Trends in Generative AI

The future of generative AI is filled with exciting possibilities and challenges as the technology continues to evolve and mature. Several key trends and prospects are likely to shape the trajectory of generative AI in the coming years.

Advancements in Model Architectures:

1. Hybrid Models: The integration of different AI architectures, such as combining GANs with Transformers or diffusion models, is likely to lead to the development of more powerful and versatile generative models. These hybrid models can leverage the strengths of each architecture to generate higher-quality and more diverse outputs, opening up new applications in areas such as creative arts, simulation, and autonomous systems.

2. Scalability and Efficiency: As generative AI models continue to grow in complexity and scale, there will be a focus on improving their efficiency and scalability. This includes the development of more efficient training algorithms, model compression techniques, and hardware accelerators that can reduce the time and cost of training large models. The ability to scale generative AI models efficiently will be critical for their widespread adoption in industry and academia.

Ethical and Responsible AI Development:

1. AI Ethics and Governance: As generative AI becomes more integrated into society, there will be an increasing emphasis on ethical and responsible AI development. This includes the establishment of AI ethics guidelines, regulatory frameworks, and governance structures to ensure that generative AI is used in ways that benefit society and minimize harm. Collaboration between AI researchers, policymakers, and industry stakeholders will be essential in shaping the future of ethical AI.

2. Transparency and Explainability: The demand for transparency and explainability in AI models will continue to grow, particularly in applications where AI decisions have significant impacts on individuals and society. Researchers are likely to focus on developing methods to make generative AI models more interpretable and transparent, allowing users to understand how AI-generated content is produced and to trust the outputs of these models.

Integration with Human Creativity:

1. Human-AI Collaboration: The future of generative AI is likely to be characterized by closer integration with human creativity, where AI serves as a tool that enhances and amplifies human creative potential. This collaborative approach can lead to the creation of new art forms, music genres, and content formats that are a blend of human and machine creativity. The development of user-friendly AI tools and interfaces will be key to enabling this collaboration and making generative AI accessible to a broader audience.

2. AI as a Creative Partner: In creative industries, AI is increasingly being viewed as a partner rather than a replacement for human creators. This partnership allows for the exploration of new creative possibilities, where AI-generated content serves as a starting point or inspiration for human artists, writers, and designers. The role of AI as a creative partner is likely to expand as the technology continues to improve and become more integrated into creative workflows.

New Applications and Use Cases:

1. Generative AI in Healthcare: The application of generative AI in healthcare is expected to grow, with new use cases emerging in areas such as drug discovery, personalized medicine, and medical imaging. AI-generated models can simulate biological processes, generate potential drug candidates, and create personalized treatment plans based on individual patient data. These applications have the potential to revolutionize healthcare by making treatments more effective and accessible.

2. Generative AI for Climate Action: Another emerging application of generative AI is in climate action, where AI models can generate solutions for environmental challenges such as carbon capture, renewable energy optimization, and sustainable agriculture. By simulating environmental scenarios and generating innovative solutions, generative AI can play a critical role in addressing the global climate crisis and promoting sustainability.

Summary

Generative AI represents a transformative technology with the potential to revolutionize various industries and aspects of society. While the possibilities are vast, it is essential to approach the development and deployment of generative AI with a focus on ethical considerations, transparency, and sustainability. By doing so, we can harness the power of generative AI to create a better and more equitable future for all.

Key Takeaways

1. **Understanding Generative AI:** Generative AI focuses on creating new content, such as text, images, and music, rather than merely analyzing existing data. It represents a significant shift in how AI can be used, offering new possibilities for creativity and innovation.

2. **Historical Evolution:** The development of generative AI has been driven by advances in deep learning, particularly with the advent of models like GANs, VAEs, and Transformers. These models have enabled AI systems to generate content with remarkable realism and creativity.

3. **Industry Impact:** Generative AI is transforming various industries, including healthcare, finance, entertainment, and manufacturing. Its ability to generate new content and solutions is leading to breakthroughs in these fields, making it a powerful tool for innovation.

4. **Ethical Considerations:** As generative AI becomes more prevalent, it raises important ethical questions, particularly around issues like bias, misinformation, and privacy. Addressing these challenges will be crucial to ensuring the responsible use of this technology.

5. **Future Prospects:** The future of generative AI holds exciting possibilities, with ongoing advancements in model architectures, ethical AI development, and new applications. As the technology continues to evolve, it is poised to play an increasingly important role in shaping the future of many industries.

Chapter 02: Key Concepts and Terminologies

Introduction

To effectively grasp the intricacies of generative AI, it is essential to understand the core concepts and terminologies that underpin this rapidly evolving field. This chapter provides a comprehensive overview of these foundational ideas, including deep learning and neural networks, supervised and unsupervised learning, generative models, and common algorithms in generative AI. By delving into these topics, readers will gain a solid foundation for understanding how generative AI systems are built and how they function.

Deep Learning and Neural Networks

Deep Learning is a subset of machine learning that focuses on neural networks with multiple layers, known as Deep Neural Networks (DNNs). These networks are designed to automatically learn and model complex patterns in data through a hierarchical representation.

Neural Networks: The basic building block of deep learning is the neural network, which mimics the way the human brain processes information. Neural networks consist of:

- **Neurons:** Nodes that perform calculations on input data. Each neuron applies an activation function to the weighted sum of its inputs.
- **Layers:** Composed of multiple neurons, layers can be classified as:
  - **Input Layer:** Receives the raw input data and forwards it to the subsequent layers.
  - **Hidden Layers:** Perform intermediate computations and feature extractions. The depth and configuration of hidden layers influence the model's ability to capture complex patterns.
  - **Output Layer:** Produces the final output or prediction based on the processed data from the hidden layers.

Training Neural Networks: Training involves adjusting the network's parameters to minimize the difference between predicted and actual outputs. This process uses:

- **Backpropagation:** A method for computing gradients of the loss function with respect to each weight. It updates weights through optimization algorithms like **Stochastic Gradient Descent (SGD)** or **Adam**.
- **Epochs:** The number of complete passes through the training dataset. Multiple epochs are required for effective learning.

Applications in Generative AI: Neural networks are pivotal in generative AI. For instance, Generative Adversarial Networks (GANs) use two neural networks—a generator and a discriminator—that compete to create realistic data. The generator aims to produce data indistinguishable from real data, while the discriminator evaluates the authenticity of generated data.

Supervised vs. Unsupervised Learning

AI models learn from data through various learning paradigms. **Supervised** and **unsupervised learning** are the two primary methods, each with distinct characteristics and applications.

Supervised Learning: In supervised learning, models are trained on labeled data, where each input is paired with a corresponding output label. The model learns to map inputs to the correct outputs.

- **Classification:** Tasks that involve categorizing input data into predefined classes. Examples include image recognition (e.g., identifying objects in photos) and spam detection in emails.
- **Regression:** Tasks that predict continuous values from input data. Examples include predicting house prices based on features like size and location.

Supervised learning is effective when the goal is to develop models that make accurate predictions based on historical data.

Unsupervised Learning: In unsupervised learning, models are trained on unlabeled data, aiming to identify patterns or structures within the data.

- **Clustering:** Grouping similar data points based on their features. Examples include customer segmentation in marketing and grouping similar news articles.
- **Dimensionality Reduction:** Reducing the number of features while preserving essential information. Techniques like **Principal Component Analysis (PCA)** help visualize high-dimensional data.

Unsupervised learning is useful for discovering hidden patterns and relationships in data without predefined labels.

Application in Generative AI: Generative AI often leverages both supervised and unsupervised learning. For example, Variational Autoencoders (VAEs) use unsupervised learning to model data distributions, while Conditional GANs (cGANs) apply supervised learning by guiding data generation with specific labels.

Generative Models: An Overview

Generative models aim to produce new data samples that resemble a given dataset. Unlike discriminative models, which focus on classifying or predicting data, generative models learn the underlying data distribution and generate new instances from it.

Types of Generative Models:

Generative Adversarial Networks (GANs): GANs consist of two neural networks—the generator and the discriminator—that are trained together. The generator creates synthetic data, and the discriminator evaluates its authenticity. The generator improves by trying to deceive the discriminator, leading to increasingly realistic outputs.

Variational Autoencoders (VAEs): VAEs encode data into a latent space—a compressed representation—and then decode it to reconstruct the original data. By sampling from this latent space, VAEs can generate new data similar to the training set.

Autoregressive Models: These models generate data sequentially, with each step dependent on the previous steps. Examples include **PixelCNN**, which generates images pixel by pixel, and **WaveNet**, which generates audio samples frame by frame.

Transformers: Originally developed for natural language processing, transformers have been adapted for generative tasks. **Generative Pre-trained Transformers (GPT)**, such as GPT-3, generate text by predicting subsequent words based on prior context. Transformers are also used for image and audio generation tasks.

Applications: Generative models have diverse applications, including:

- **Image Synthesis:** Creating realistic images, enhancing artistic creativity, and generating new designs.

- **Text Generation:** Producing coherent and contextually relevant text for content creation, chatbots, and language translation.
- **Music Composition:** Generating original music compositions and enhancing the creative process.
- **Scientific Simulations:** Modeling complex systems and generating synthetic data for research and experimentation.

Common Algorithms in Generative AI

Several algorithms and techniques are commonly employed in generative AI, each with unique strengths and applications:

1. Generative Adversarial Networks (GANs)

GANs are highly effective for generating realistic images, videos, and other data types. The adversarial setup—where the generator and discriminator compete—drives the generator to create increasingly convincing data.

Use Cases: GANs are particularly effective for generating realistic images, videos, and other data types. Their ability to produce high-quality and convincing results makes them suitable for applications such as:

- **Image Synthesis:** Creating photorealistic images of people, landscapes, and objects, useful in entertainment, fashion, and digital art.
- **Video Generation:** Generating video content for simulations, training data, or content creation.
- **Data Augmentation:** Enhancing datasets with additional samples to improve the performance of machine learning models.
- **Style Transfer:** Applying artistic styles to images, creating novel visual effects for applications in media and advertising.

2. Variational Autoencoders (VAEs)

VAEs are used for generating data by learning a probabilistic latent space. They excel at creating diverse and high-quality samples, making them suitable for tasks like image and text generation.

Use Cases: VAEs excel at generating diverse and high-quality samples by learning a probabilistic latent space. Their applications include:

- **Image Generation:** Producing diverse images based on learned data distributions, used in creative industries for design and art.
- **Text Generation:** Creating varied text samples for natural language processing tasks like chatbots and content generation.
- **Anomaly Detection:** Identifying outliers in data by comparing generated samples to observed data, applicable in fraud detection and quality control.
- **Data Compression:** Reducing data dimensions while retaining essential features, useful in efficient storage and transmission.

3. Reinforcement Learning (RL)

While not a generative model itself, RL can be used in generative tasks where an agent learns to generate sequences of actions or decisions. RL is applied in areas such as game playing and robotic control.

Use Cases: Although not a generative model per se, RL can be applied in generative tasks where an agent learns to generate sequences of actions or decisions. Key applications include:

- **Game Playing:** Training agents to generate optimal strategies and behaviors in complex games, such as chess or video games.
- **Robotic Control:** Enabling robots to learn and generate sequences of movements for tasks like assembly, navigation, and manipulation.
- **Interactive Systems:** Developing systems that adapt and generate responses based on user interactions, such as personalized recommendation engines.

4. Transformers

Transformers, with their self-attention mechanisms, have revolutionized natural language processing and are now applied to other domains. Models like GPT-3 set new benchmarks for generating human-like text and have been adapted for image and audio generation.

Use Cases: Transformers, known for their self-attention mechanisms, have transformed natural language processing and are applied to other domains. Examples include:

- **Text Generation:** Models like GPT-3 create coherent and contextually relevant text, useful in content creation, translation, and conversational agents.
- **Image Generation:** Adapting transformer architectures to generate images, enhancing creative and design processes.
- **Audio Generation:** Producing high-quality audio samples, including music and speech synthesis, applicable in media and entertainment.
- **Multimodal Applications:** Combining text, image, and audio generation for comprehensive content creation solutions.

5. Autoregressive Models

These models generate data step by step, with each element conditioned on previous ones. They are effective for tasks involving sequences, such as text, music, and speech generation. Examples include **PixelCNN** for images and **WaveNet** for audio.

Use Cases: Autoregressive models generate data sequentially, conditioning each element on previous ones. Their effectiveness is seen in:

- **Text Generation:** Producing coherent and contextually relevant text sequences for applications in writing assistance and storytelling, as seen in models like GPT-2.
- **Music Composition:** Generating music sequences that mimic styles or genres, useful in music production and composition tools.

- **Speech Synthesis:** Creating realistic and natural-sounding speech applicable to virtual assistants and accessibility tools.
- **Image Generation:** Generating high-quality images pixel by pixel, used in artistic creation and visual effects.

6. Diffusion Models

An emerging approach, diffusion models generate high-quality data by gradually denoising a random signal. They have shown promise in producing detailed and realistic samples, particularly in image generation.

Use Cases: Diffusion models, an emerging approach, generate high-quality data by progressively denoising random signals. Their applications include:

- **Image Generation:** Producing detailed and realistic images with potential uses in high-resolution art and design.
- **Data Reconstruction:** Reconstructing corrupted or incomplete data, applicable in image restoration and enhancement.
- **Simulations:** Creating synthetic data for complex simulations in scientific research and virtual environments.

Summary

This chapter has provided an in-depth exploration of the key concepts and terminologies essential for understanding generative AI. By examining deep learning and neural networks, the distinctions between supervised and unsupervised learning, the various types of generative models, and the common algorithms used in this field, we have laid the groundwork for a deeper understanding of how generative AI systems function. These foundational concepts will be instrumental as you continue to explore and apply generative AI technologies in subsequent chapters.

Generative AI

Key Takeaways

Deep Learning and Neural Networks:

- Deep learning employs neural networks with multiple layers (DNNs) to model complex data patterns, inspired by the brain's structure.
- Neural networks are organized in layers (input, hidden, output) and are trained using backpropagation to minimize errors.
- They play a crucial role in generative AI, enabling realistic data creation through models like GANs.

Supervised vs. Unsupervised Learning:

- **Supervised Learning:** Trains models on labeled data to map inputs to known outputs, used in tasks such as classification and regression.
- **Unsupervised Learning:** Trains models on unlabeled data to find patterns and structures, employed in clustering and dimensionality reduction.
- Both paradigms are vital in generative AI, with unsupervised learning often used for modeling data distributions and supervised learning guiding specific generative processes.

Generative Models:

Generative models create new data samples resembling the training data by learning the data distribution.

- **Generative Adversarial Networks (GANs):** Feature a generator and discriminator in a competitive setup to produce highly realistic data.
- **Variational Autoencoders (VAEs):** Encode data into a latent space and decode it to generate new samples, focusing on probabilistic representations.
- **Autoregressive Models:** Generate data sequentially, conditioning each step on previous data, effective for sequences like text and audio.

- **Transformers:** Originally for NLP, adapted for generative tasks in text, image, and audio domains.

Common Algorithms in Generative AI:

- **GANs:** Innovate realistic data generation through adversarial training.
- **VAEs:** Offer diverse sample generation via probabilistic latent spaces.
- **Reinforcement Learning (RL):** Generates sequences of actions or decisions, useful in game playing and robotics.
- **Autoregressive Models:** Predict each element in a sequence based on prior elements suitable for text, music, and speech.
- **Diffusion Models:** Emerging technique for high-quality data generation by progressively denoising random signals, showing promise in detailed image creation.

Part II: Generative Models and Techniques

Chapter 03: Generative Adversarial Networks (GANs)

Introduction

Generative Adversarial Networks (GANs) represent a pivotal advancement in artificial intelligence, particularly in the field of generative models. This chapter provides an in-depth exploration of GANs, including their foundational principles, operational mechanics, various types, and practical applications.

Introduction to GANs

Generative Adversarial Networks (GANs) were introduced in 2014 by Ian Goodfellow and his team as a novel framework for generating synthetic data. GANs have since become a cornerstone of generative AI, offering a unique approach to data generation through adversarial training.

Foundational Concept

Adversarial training lies at the core of GANs. This involves two neural networks—the **generator** and the **discriminator**—engaged in a competitive game. The generator creates synthetic data samples from random noise while the discriminator evaluates these samples against real data. The generator's goal is to produce data that the discriminator cannot distinguish from real data, whereas the discriminator aims to become increasingly adept at differentiating between real and fake data.

Adversarial Setup

This adversarial setup creates a feedback loop where both networks improve iteratively. As the generator becomes better at creating realistic data, the discriminator becomes more skilled at detecting subtle differences. This ongoing interaction drives the generator to produce higher-quality data and ensures that the discriminator remains a robust evaluator.

Impact and Significance

GANs have revolutionized the ability to generate synthetic data that closely mimics real-world data. This has profound implications across various fields, including computer vision, natural language processing, and creative industries, by enabling the creation of highly realistic and diverse data samples.

How GANs Work: The Generator and Discriminator

The architecture of GANs consists of two main components: the generator and the discriminator. Each plays a critical role in the adversarial process.

The Generator:

- **Function:** The generator takes a latent vector, which is a vector of random noise, and transforms it into a data sample. This transformation is accomplished through a series of neural network layers that progressively refine the random noise into a structured output.
- **Objective:** The primary goal of the generator is to produce data samples that resemble the real data distribution as closely as possible. The generator's success is measured by how effectively it can "fool" the discriminator into believing that its synthetic samples are real.

- **Training:** During training, the generator receives feedback from the discriminator, which helps it adjust its parameters to improve the quality of the generated data. The feedback is based on how well the discriminator can distinguish between real and fake samples.

The Discriminator:

- **Function:** The discriminator is a binary classifier that evaluates data samples and determines their authenticity. It receives both real data from the training set and fake data from the generator and outputs a probability score indicating whether the sample is real or fake.
- **Objective:** The discriminator's goal is to accurately classify data samples as real or fake. It provides valuable feedback to the generator, guiding it in producing increasingly convincing data.
- **Training:** The discriminator is trained to minimize its classification error, improving its ability to detect fake data while distinguishing it from real data. This continuous improvement pushes the generator to enhance its data generation capabilities.

Training Process:

GANs are trained using a two-step process:

- **Step 1:** The discriminator is updated first. It is presented with a batch of real and fake samples and trained to maximize its ability to correctly classify them.
- **Step 2:** The generator is updated next. It generates a new batch of fake samples and is trained based on the feedback from the discriminator. The generator's objective is to produce samples that the discriminator classifies as real.
- **Iterative Improvement:** This training process is repeated iteratively, with both networks improving their performance based on the feedback received. The generator and discriminator continue to evolve until the generator produces

data that the discriminator can no longer reliably distinguish from real data.

Types of GANs

Several variations of GANs have been developed to address specific challenges and extend the capabilities of the original GAN framework. Each type introduces unique features and applications:

Deep Convolutional GAN (DCGAN):

Overview

DCGANs leverage deep convolutional neural networks (CNNs) for both the generator and discriminator. This architecture is particularly effective for generating high-quality images due to its ability to capture spatial hierarchies and features.

Key Features

DCGANs use convolutional layers in the generator to produce detailed images and deep convolutional layers in the discriminator to enhance its ability to detect subtle differences between real and fake images. This combination allows DCGANs to generate high-resolution images with greater fidelity.

Applications

DCGANs are commonly used in tasks that involve image generation, such as creating realistic photographs of faces, objects, or scenes. They have applications in areas like art, entertainment, and virtual reality, where high-quality image generation is essential.

StyleGAN:

Overview

StyleGAN, developed by NVIDIA, introduces a style-based generator architecture that enables fine-grained control over generated images. It allows for manipulation of various aspects of the generated images, such as style and attributes, at different levels of detail.

Key Features

StyleGAN incorporates a style transfer mechanism that enables users to modify specific attributes of images, such as facial expressions, hairstyles, or artistic effects. This feature provides a high degree of flexibility in image generation.

Applications

StyleGAN is widely used in generating high-resolution images for applications such as creating avatars, virtual characters, and artistic portraits. It is also employed in fashion and design industries for generating clothing designs and visual content.

CycleGAN:

Overview

CycleGAN focuses on unpaired image-to-image translation, allowing for the transformation of images from one domain to another without requiring paired examples. This approach is valuable for tasks where paired training data is not available.

Key Features

CycleGAN uses a cycle-consistency loss to ensure that images translated from one domain to another can be transformed back to their original domain. This process preserves the content while altering the style or appearance.

Applications

CycleGAN is used in tasks such as style transfer, domain adaptation, and image-to-image translation. Examples include converting photographs to artistic styles, translating images between different weather conditions, and mapping images from one visual domain to another.

Applications of GANs

GANs have found a wide range of applications across various domains due to their ability to generate realistic and diverse data. Here are some notable applications:

Image Generation

- **Realistic Images:** GANs can generate highly realistic images of people, objects, and scenes. This capability has significant applications in advertising, entertainment, and virtual reality, where realistic imagery is crucial for engaging content.
- **Data Augmentation:** GANs can create synthetic data to augment existing training datasets. This is particularly useful for improving the performance of machine learning models in tasks such as image classification, object detection, and facial recognition.

Video Generation

- **Deepfake Technology:** GANs are used to create deepfake videos, which involve manipulating existing footage to generate realistic yet synthetic videos of people. This technology has implications for media, entertainment, and security, enabling the creation of convincing video content for various purposes.

Art and Design

- **Creative Tools:** GANs assist artists and designers in creating novel and aesthetically pleasing artwork, styles, and designs. They enable the exploration of new creative possibilities, allowing for the generation of unique art pieces and design concepts.

Medical Imaging:

- **Image Enhancement:** GANs enhance medical images by improving resolution, denoising, and generating synthetic medical data for research and training. This capability aids in medical diagnostics, research, and the development of new imaging techniques.

Text-to-Image Synthesis:

- **Visual Representation:** GANs can generate images from textual descriptions, allowing for the creation of visual content based on written input. This technology has applications in content creation, assistive technologies, and virtual environments where visual representation of textual information is needed.

Fashion and Retail:

- **Virtual Try-Ons:** GANs are used to create virtual try-on systems that allow users to see how clothing or accessories would look on them before making a purchase. This enhances the online shopping experience by providing realistic visualizations of products.

Summary

Generative Adversarial Networks (GANs) have emerged as a transformative technology in generative AI, offering a powerful framework for generating high-quality and diverse data. By understanding the foundational principles, operational mechanisms, various types of GANs, and their wide-ranging applications, we can appreciate the impact of GANs across different industries and explore their potential for future advancements in data generation and manipulation. As GANs continue to evolve, they will undoubtedly play a pivotal role in shaping the future of AI-driven creativity and innovation.

Key Takeaways

> **GAN Fundamentals:** Generative Adversarial Networks (GANs) consist of two neural networks—the generator and the discriminator—that engage in an adversarial training process. The generator creates synthetic data, while the discriminator evaluates and distinguishes between real and fake data, driving improvements in both networks.
>
> **Mechanics of GANs:** The generator transforms random noise into structured data samples, while the discriminator assesses the authenticity of these samples. Training involves iterative feedback loops where both networks enhance their performance, leading to the generation of increasingly realistic data.
>
> **Types of GANs:**
>
> - **Deep Convolutional GANs (DCGANs):** Utilize convolutional neural networks to generate high-resolution images, effective in tasks like image generation and augmentation.
> - **StyleGAN:** Introduces a style-based generator for fine-grained control over generated images, useful in applications such as creating avatars, artistic portraits, and fashion designs.
> - **CycleGAN:** Facilitates unpaired image-to-image translation, enabling transformations between different visual domains without requiring paired datasets, ideal for style transfer and domain adaptation tasks.
>
> **Applications of GANs:**
>
> - **Image Generation:** GANs produce highly realistic images for various industries, including advertising, virtual reality, and data augmentation.
> - **Video Generation:** GANs enable the creation of deepfake videos with applications in media, entertainment, and security.

- **Art and Design:** Assist artists and designers in generating unique artwork and designs, exploring new creative possibilities.
- **Medical Imaging:** Enhance medical images and generate synthetic medical data, supporting diagnostics and research.
- **Text-to-Image Synthesis:** Convert textual descriptions into visual content, useful in content creation and virtual environments.
- **Fashion and Retail:** Provide virtual try-on systems for online shopping, improving the customer experience with realistic product visualizations.

Chapter 04: Variational Autoencoders (VAEs)

Introduction

Variational Autoencoders (VAEs) represent a sophisticated class of generative models that have become fundamental in modern machine learning and artificial intelligence. This chapter provides an in-depth exploration of VAEs, delving into their core components, the concept of latent space representation, and their broad range of applications in generating images and data.

Introduction to VAEs

Variational Autoencoders (VAEs) are generative models that integrate autoencoders with probabilistic graphical models, offering a unique approach to learning and generating data. VAEs are distinguished by their ability to generate new, coherent data samples by learning a compact, probabilistic representation of the input data. They are based on principles from Bayesian inference, where the goal is to approximate complex data distributions.

Historical Context and Development

VAEs were introduced by Kingma and Welling in 2013 as a way to overcome the limitations of traditional autoencoders. Traditional autoencoders learn deterministic mappings from input data to a lower-dimensional latent space, which can limit their generative capabilities. VAEs extend this concept by learning a probabilistic mapping, allowing for richer and more diverse data generation.

Architectural Components:

Encoder Network:

The encoder, also known as the inference network, compresses input data into a probabilistic latent space. It outputs parameters (mean and variance) of a probability distribution for each data point rather than a fixed latent code.

Latent Space:

This latent space is a continuous, lower-dimensional representation of the data where similar data points are located close to each other. It allows the model to capture underlying data structures and variations.

Decoder Network:

The decoder, or generative network, samples from the latent space and reconstructs the original input data. It transforms the latent representation back into the data space, aiming to produce outputs that resemble the original data.

Training Process:

Variational Inference:

VAEs use variational inference to approximate complex posterior distributions. This approach involves optimizing the evidence lower bound (ELBO) to find the best approximation to the true posterior distribution.

- **Loss Function:** The loss function of a VAE consists of two main parts: the reconstruction loss and the KL divergence loss. The reconstruction loss measures the difference between the original input and the reconstructed output, while the KL divergence loss regularizes the latent space to follow a standard Gaussian distribution.

Latent Space Representation

Latent Space Representation is a key concept in VAEs that defines how data is encoded into a compressed, probabilistic format. This representation is essential for generating new data samples and understanding the structure of the data.

Encoding Data:

- **Probabilistic Mapping:** The encoder maps each data point to a distribution in the latent space rather than a fixed point. This distribution is typically modeled as a Gaussian with mean and variance parameters.
- **Reparameterization Trick:** To enable backpropagation and gradient-based optimization, VAEs use the reparameterization trick. This involves expressing the latent variables as a deterministic function of the mean, variance, and sample from a standard Gaussian distribution.

Sampling from Latent Space:

- **Diverse Sampling:** By sampling from the learned latent distribution, VAEs can generate diverse and varied data samples. This sampling process introduces randomness, allowing the model to produce new instances that reflect the learned data distribution.
- **Exploring Latent Space:** Visualization of the latent space can provide insights into how the model captures data variations. Techniques such as t-SNE or PCA can be used to project the latent space into 2D or 3D for better interpretability.

Regularization and Structure:

- **KL Divergence Regularization:** The KL divergence loss term ensures that the latent space is well-structured and follows a known distribution (usually a standard Gaussian). This regularization prevents the latent space from becoming disorganized and promotes smooth transitions between latent variables.

Applications of VAEs in Image and Data Generation

Variational Autoencoders have diverse and impactful applications due to their ability to learn and generate complex data distributions. Here are some key areas where VAEs are effectively employed:

Image Generation:
High-Quality Image Synthesis

VAEs are used to generate new images that resemble the training data. For instance, they can create realistic portraits, artwork, or designs by sampling from the latent space and decoding the samples.

Image Editing and Manipulation

VAEs enable various image editing tasks, such as altering attributes (e.g., changing facial expressions or hairstyles) or combining features from different images. By manipulating the latent space, users can achieve targeted modifications in generated images.

Image Super-Resolution

VAEs can enhance image resolution by generating high-resolution versions from low-resolution inputs. This application is valuable in improving image quality for applications like medical imaging and satellite imagery.

Data Augmentation:

Synthetic Data Creation

VAEs generate synthetic data for training machine learning models, especially when real data is limited or sensitive. This augmentation improves model performance and generalization by providing additional diverse examples.

Imputation of Missing Data

VAEs can impute missing or corrupted data by reconstructing it from the latent representation. This capability is useful in scenarios where data is incomplete or noisy.

Text and Speech Generation:

Text Generation

VAEs adapted for text generation learn to encode and generate coherent text sequences. They are used for creating diverse and contextually relevant sentences or paragraphs in applications like chatbots or creative writing.

Speech Synthesis

VAEs can generate synthetic speech by learning representations of audio signals. This technology is applied in text-to-speech systems, voice cloning, and creating diverse voice samples for virtual assistants.

Anomaly Detection:

Detecting Outliers

VAEs learn the normal data distribution and can identify anomalies or outliers by detecting deviations from the learned distribution. This application is useful in fraud detection, network security, and quality control.

Data Compression and Denoising:

Data Compression

VAEs can compress data into a lower-dimensional latent space, reducing storage and computational requirements. This compression is useful for efficient data storage and transmission.

Denoising

VAEs can learn to reconstruct clean data from noisy inputs, effectively denoising data. This application is valuable in enhancing data quality in various fields, including image processing and audio enhancement.

Summary

Variational Autoencoders (VAEs) represent a powerful and versatile approach to generative modeling, combining the strengths of autoencoders and probabilistic methods. By learning a probabilistic representation of data, VAEs enable the generation of diverse and high-quality samples across various domains. Their ability to model complex data distributions and produce realistic outputs makes them invaluable tools in fields ranging from image and text generation to anomaly detection and data augmentation.

The flexibility and effectiveness of VAEs in addressing a wide range of tasks highlight their significance in advancing the capabilities of generative AI. As research and development continue, VAEs are likely to play an increasingly prominent role in solving complex problems and enabling innovative applications in artificial intelligence.

Key Takeaways

> **Variational Autoencoders (VAEs)** are advanced generative models that use probabilistic methods to encode and generate data, providing a powerful approach to creating diverse and realistic samples.

Latent Space Representation is central to VAEs, allowing for the encoding of data into a compressed, probabilistic format and enabling the generation of new, varied samples through sampling and decoding.

Applications of VAEs span a wide range of domains, including image generation, data augmentation, text and speech synthesis, anomaly detection, and data compression. VAEs offer versatile solutions for various tasks by leveraging their ability to model complex data distributions and generate high-quality outputs.

Chapter 05: Transformer Models

Introduction

Transformers have revolutionized the field of natural language processing (NLP) and have extended their influence to other domains, including computer vision and audio processing. Their unique architecture and mechanisms have set new standards for model performance, leading to significant advancements in generative AI and machine learning. This chapter delves into the fundamentals of transformer models, focusing on their introduction, the attention mechanism, key variants such as GPT, and other prominent transformer-based models like BERT.

Introduction to Transformers

Transformers were introduced by Vaswani et al. in the seminal paper "Attention is All You Need" (2017) and have since become the cornerstone of modern NLP. Unlike previous sequence-to-sequence models that relied on recurrent neural networks (RNNs) or convolutional neural networks (CNNs), transformers leverage self-attention mechanisms to handle dependencies between tokens in a sequence more efficiently.

Architectural Overview

Encoder-Decoder Structure

The original transformer model consists of an encoder-decoder architecture. The encoder processes input sequences and transforms them into a continuous representation, while the decoder generates output sequences from this representation.

Layers

Both the encoder and decoder are composed of multiple layers. Each encoder layer has two sub-layers: a multi-head self-attention mechanism and a feed-forward neural network. Each decoder layer includes an additional sub-layer for cross-attention, which attends to the encoder's output.

Positional Encoding

Since transformers do not inherently understand the order of tokens, positional encodings are added to input embeddings to provide information about token positions in the sequence.

Advantages:

- **Parallelization:** Unlike RNNs, transformers allow for parallel processing of input sequences, leading to faster training times.
- **Long-Range Dependencies:** Self-attention enables transformers to capture long-range dependencies between tokens more effectively than RNNs or CNNs.

Attention Mechanism

The attention mechanism is the core innovation of transformer models, allowing them to weigh the importance of different tokens in a sequence dynamically.

Self-Attention:

Mechanism

Self-attention computes attention scores for each token with respect to every other token in the sequence. This results in a weighted representation where tokens are compared and combined based on their relevance.

Scaled Dot-Product Attention

This approach calculates attention scores by taking the dot product of query and key vectors, scaling by the square root of the dimension, and applying a softmax function to obtain attention weights.

Multi-Head Attention

Multi-head attention extends self-attention by running multiple attention mechanisms in parallel, allowing the model to capture different aspects of token relationships.

Cross-Attention:

Purpose

In the decoder, cross-attention allows tokens to attend to the encoder's output, facilitating the generation of sequences based on the input representation.

Mechanism

Similar to self-attention, but instead of attending to the same sequence, the decoder attends to the encoder's output.

Benefits:

- **Dynamic Contextualization:** Attention mechanisms enable transformers to dynamically focus on relevant parts of the sequence, improving contextual understanding and representation.

- **Improved Performance:** By leveraging attention, transformers achieve state-of-the-art performance on various NLP tasks and benchmarks.

GPT (Generative Pre-trained Transformers) and its Variants

Generative Pre-trained Transformers (GPT) represent a series of groundbreaking models developed by OpenAI, designed to generate coherent, contextually relevant text based on extensive pre-training and fine-tuning techniques. These models are built on transformer architecture, which excels in handling sequential data and capturing long-range dependencies in text.

GPT-1

Introduction
GPT-1 was the pioneering model in the GPT series, introduced in 2018. It marked a significant advancement by introducing the concept of pre-training a model on a large corpus of text before fine-tuning it on specific tasks. This approach helped GPT-1 leverage general language understanding to perform a variety of NLP tasks.

Architecture
GPT-1 is built on a stack of transformer decoder layers. It employs causal (autoregressive) attention, meaning it generates text sequentially, predicting the next word in a sequence based on previous words. This architecture allows GPT-1 to handle diverse text generation tasks with reasonable coherence.

GPT-2

Scaling Up
Released in 2019, GPT-2 represents a substantial increase in model size and training data compared to GPT-1. With 1.5 billion parameters, GPT-2's expanded capacity allows it to generate more detailed and contextually accurate text. The increase in parameters and training data improved its ability to handle complex language tasks.

Capabilities

GPT-2 can generate long, coherent passages of text, complete partial sentences, answer questions, and perform various NLP tasks with minimal fine-tuning. Its ability to generate contextually relevant content across different domains makes it a versatile tool for text generation and analysis.

GPT-3

Revolutionary Scale

GPT-3, introduced in 2020, is one of the largest language models to date, featuring an astounding 175 billion parameters. This massive scale enables GPT-3 to perform a broad array of language tasks with minimal task-specific training. Its size allows it to understand and generate text with impressive fluency and depth.

Few-Shot Learning

GPT-3 is notable for its few-shot learning capabilities. It can perform tasks by learning from just a few examples provided in the prompt, demonstrating its ability to generalize from limited input. This characteristic significantly enhances its flexibility and usability across various applications.

GPT-4 and Beyond

Advancements

Subsequent versions, including GPT-4, continue to build upon the successes of earlier models. GPT-4 incorporates improvements in model architecture, training techniques, and fine-tuning strategies, addressing limitations observed in previous iterations. These advancements contribute to even more accurate, nuanced, and contextually aware text generation.

Future Prospects

As the field of generative AI evolves, future versions of GPT models are expected to further enhance their capabilities, incorporating innovations in AI research and expanding their potential applications. Continued advancements in training methods, model scalability, and fine-tuning approaches will likely drive the next generation of GPT technologies.

BERT and Other Transformer-Based Models

Transformer-based models have revolutionized the field of natural language processing (NLP) by introducing new paradigms in language understanding and representation. These models leverage advanced techniques to capture context, improve performance, and address various limitations of earlier models. Below is an in-depth look at BERT and several key transformer-based models that have significantly impacted the field.

BERT (Bidirectional Encoder Representations from Transformers)

Bidirectional Context

BERT, introduced by Google in 2018, distinguishes itself by using bidirectional attention. Unlike models like GPT that generate text autoregressively, BERT analyzes context from both directions (left and right) within a sequence. This bidirectional approach enhances the model's ability to grasp the nuanced meanings of words based on their surrounding context, leading to a deeper understanding of language.

Pre-training Tasks: BERT's pre-training involves two key tasks:

- **Masked Language Modeling (MLM):** During MLM, random tokens in a sentence are masked, and the model learns to predict these masked tokens based on the context provided by the other tokens. This task helps BERT develop a robust understanding of word relationships and context.
- **Next Sentence Prediction (NSP):** NSP involves predicting whether one sentence logically follows another. This task aids BERT in understanding the relationship between sentences, which is crucial for tasks like question answering and natural language inference.

Applications

BERT has set new benchmarks in various NLP tasks, including question answering (e.g., SQuAD), named entity recognition (NER), and natural language inference (NLI). Its ability to understand context and relationships between sentences has made it a foundational model in modern NLP applications.

RoBERTa (Robustly optimized BERT approach)

Optimizations

RoBERTa, developed by Facebook AI, builds on BERT's architecture with several optimizations:

- **Removal of NSP Task:** RoBERTa eliminates the NSP task, which was found to contribute little to the model's performance.
- **Increased Training Data and Duration:** RoBERTa is trained on more data and for a longer period, allowing it to capture more nuanced language patterns.
- **Dynamic Masking:** It uses dynamic masking during training, where tokens are randomly masked and unmasked in each epoch, enhancing the model's ability to generalize.

These changes result in RoBERTa achieving superior performance on a range of NLP benchmarks compared to the original BERT model.

DistilBERT

Model Compression

DistilBERT is a distilled version of BERT, created through knowledge distillation—a technique where a smaller model is trained to replicate the performance of a larger model. DistilBERT maintains much of BERT's capabilities while being more computationally efficient. It is faster and requires less memory, making it suitable for deployment in resource-constrained environments.

ALBERT (A Lite BERT)

Parameter Efficiency

ALBERT focuses on reducing the model size while preserving performance:

- **Factorized Embedding Parameterization:** ALBERT reduces the number of parameters by separating the embedding matrix from the hidden layers, which decreases memory usage.
- **Cross-Layer Parameter Sharing:** It shares parameters across layers to further reduce the model size without significantly impacting performance.

These innovations make ALBERT a more parameter-efficient alternative to BERT, suitable for scenarios where computational resources are limited.

T5 (Text-To-Text Transfer Transformer)

Unified Framework

T5, developed by Google Research, adopts a unified framework where all NLP tasks are framed as text-to-text problems. This approach treats both inputs and outputs as text, simplifying the training and application of the model across a wide range of tasks, including translation, summarization, and question answering.

T5's flexibility and generalization capabilities make it a powerful tool for diverse NLP applications.

XLNet

Permutation-Based Training
XLNet addresses some limitations of BERT's bidirectional context by using a permutation-based objective for training. This approach allows the model to capture bidirectional contexts while retaining autoregressive benefits. It trains on different permutations of word sequences, which helps it understand context more effectively and improves performance on various NLP tasks.

Summary

Transformer models have revolutionized the field of artificial intelligence, particularly in natural language processing. Their innovative architecture and attention mechanisms enable them to handle complex dependencies and context effectively, setting new standards for model performance. GPT models showcase the power of generative pre-training, while BERT and its variants highlight advancements in bidirectional context understanding. As transformer models continue to evolve, they offer exciting possibilities for advancing generative AI and addressing a wide range of applications across various domains.

Key Takeaways

> **Transformers** leverage self-attention mechanisms to capture complex dependencies and context in sequences, enabling efficient and effective processing of data.
>
> **Attention Mechanisms** allow transformers to dynamically weigh the importance of different tokens, improving contextual understanding and representation.
>
> **GPT Models** excel in text generation and few-shot learning, showcasing the power of large-scale pre-training and autoregressive modeling.
>
> **BERT and its Variants** focus on bidirectional context understanding, with advancements such as RoBERTa, DistilBERT, and ALBERT enhancing performance and efficiency.
>
> **Transformers** have set new benchmarks in NLP and are expanding their applications to other domains, driving innovations and improvements in generative AI.

Chapter 06: Diffusion Models

Introduction

Diffusion models represent a cutting-edge approach in generative modeling, leveraging the concept of diffusion processes to produce high-quality data samples. This chapter delves into the principles behind diffusion models, their data generation mechanisms, and their diverse applications in image and audio generation.

Introduction to Diffusion Models

Diffusion models are inspired by physical diffusion processes where particles spread from areas of high concentration to areas of low concentration. In generative modeling, this concept is adapted to progressively convert noise into structured data through a series of steps. These models have gained attention for their ability to generate high-quality samples with remarkable detail and fidelity.

Conceptual Foundation:

Forward Diffusion Process

This phase involves adding noise to data incrementally over several steps, transforming it into a noisy distribution that approximates pure noise. This process simulates how data would become increasingly unrecognizable when subjected to noise.

Reverse Denoising Process

In this phase, a learned model is trained to reverse the noise addition process. Starting from noisy data, the model iteratively refines it to recover the original data distribution. This denoising process gradually reconstructs data from random noise.

Mathematical Formulation:

Stochastic Differential Equations (SDEs)

The forward diffusion process is often modeled using SDEs that define how noise is added over time. These equations describe the dynamics of noise addition and are central to simulating the diffusion process.

Objective Function

The training of diffusion models involves minimizing a loss function that measures the difference between the predicted and actual noise. This helps the model learn the reverse process effectively.

Training Dynamics:

Training Data

Diffusion models require large datasets to learn the noise distribution and the denoising process accurately. The training involves multiple iterations of the data to refine the model's ability to generate realistic samples.

Evaluation Metrics

Metrics such as Inception Score (IS) and Fréchet Inception Distance (FID) are used to evaluate the quality of generated samples, assessing their realism and diversity.

How Diffusion Processes Generate Data

Diffusion models generate data through a well-defined process of noise addition and denoising, which can be broken down into several stages:

Forward Diffusion Process:

Noise Addition

Data is gradually corrupted by adding Gaussian noise at each step. The noise level increases progressively, transforming the data into a state that closely resembles random noise.

Discrete Steps

The forward process is discretized into a series of steps, with each step introducing a small amount of noise. The number of steps and the noise schedule are crucial for controlling the quality of the generated data.

Reverse Denoising Process:

Denoising Network

A neural network, often a variant of U-Net or a similar architecture, is trained to predict and remove noise from corrupted data. The network learns to approximate the reverse diffusion process by minimizing the difference between predicted and actual noise.

Sampling Procedure

To generate new samples, the model starts with pure noise and applies the learned denoising function iteratively. Each step refines the noise into structured data, resulting in coherent and high-quality samples.

Advanced Techniques:

Conditional Diffusion Models

These models generate data conditioned on additional inputs, such as text descriptions or labels. By incorporating conditioning information, the models can produce samples that adhere to specific constraints or prompts.

Diffusion-Based Super-Resolution

Diffusion models are used to enhance the resolution of images by generating high-resolution details from low-resolution inputs. This application leverages the model's ability to learn fine-grained details through the denoising process.

Applications in Image and Audio Generation

Diffusion models have shown impressive results in generating high-quality images and audio. Their ability to produce realistic and diverse samples has expanded their applications across various fields.

Image Generation

High-Resolution and Realistic Images

Diffusion models are capable of generating detailed and high-resolution images, capturing intricate textures and structures. These models have set new standards for image quality in generative AI.

Conditional Image Generation

Models like DALL-E and Imagen use diffusion processes to generate images based on textual descriptions or other inputs. This capability enables the creation of images that align with specific prompts or themes.

Inpainting and Editing

Diffusion models can be applied to image inpainting and editing tasks, where missing or corrupted parts of an image are filled in or modified based on the surrounding context.

Audio Generation

High-Fidelity Audio

Diffusion models have demonstrated their ability to generate high-fidelity audio, including speech and music. These models simulate the diffusion of noise in audio signals, producing realistic and natural-sounding outputs.

Speech Synthesis

Models such as DiffWave use diffusion processes for synthesizing speech with natural prosody and clarity. This application is valuable for creating realistic voice clones and enhancing text-to-speech systems.

Music Composition

Diffusion models are used to generate complex musical compositions by learning to reverse the diffusion of noise in audio signals. This approach offers new possibilities for creative music generation and sound design.

Summary

Diffusion models represent a significant advancement in generative modeling, offering a novel approach to data generation by simulating diffusion processes. Their ability to produce high-quality images and audio has set new benchmarks in generative AI, making them a powerful tool for various applications. By learning to reverse the diffusion of noise, these models provide a robust framework for generating realistic and diverse samples, driving innovation in both creative and practical domains.

Key Takeaways

> **Diffusion Models** utilize a forward diffusion process (noise addition) and a reverse denoising process (noise removal) to generate high-quality data samples.
>
> **Forward Diffusion Process** gradually corrupts data with noise, creating a noisy distribution used for learning the data distribution.
>
> **Reverse Denoising Process** involves training a neural network to reverse the diffusion process, generating coherent data from random noise.
>
> **Applications** of diffusion models include high-resolution image generation, conditional image creation, and high-fidelity audio synthesis, with promising results across various domains.
>
> **Advanced Techniques** such as conditional diffusion models and diffusion-based super-resolution further enhance the versatility and applicability of diffusion models in generative AI.

Part III: Applications of Generative AI

Chapter 07: Text Generation

Introduction

Text generation has become a pivotal aspect of natural language processing (NLP), leveraging sophisticated models to create coherent and contextually relevant text. This chapter explores key language models driving text generation, examines their applications, and discusses the implications of their use, including ethical considerations.

Language Models: GPT, BERT, T5

Language models are the cornerstone of text generation, utilizing deep learning techniques to understand and generate human-like text. This section explores three influential language models: GPT, BERT, and T5.

GPT (Generative Pre-trained Transformer)

Overview:

Developed by OpenAI, GPT is a series of models that use a transformer-based architecture to generate human-like text. GPT-3, the third iteration, has 175 billion parameters, making it one of the most powerful language models to date. Its vast scale enables it to perform a wide range of language tasks with impressive accuracy.

Architecture:

GPT utilizes a unidirectional transformer architecture, where the model predicts the next word in a sequence based on the preceding words. This autoregressive approach enables the generation of coherent and contextually relevant text.

Training and Capabilities:

GPT is pre-trained on a diverse dataset from the internet, which allows it to understand a wide range of topics and generate text across various domains. It excels in tasks such as text completion, translation, summarization, and creative writing. For example, GPT-3 can write essays, generate poetry, and even simulate characters in interactive narratives.

Applications:

GPT has been used in various applications, including content creation for blogs and articles, generating creative writing such as poetry and stories, and assisting in code generation for programming tasks.

BERT (Bidirectional Encoder Representations from Transformers)

Overview:

Developed by Google, BERT represents a significant advancement in understanding the context of words in a sentence. Unlike GPT, which processes text in one direction, BERT uses a bidirectional approach to capture context from both sides of a word.

Architecture:

BERT's transformer architecture includes multiple layers of bidirectional attention mechanisms. It uses two main pre-training tasks: masked language modeling (where some words in a sentence are masked, and the model predicts them) and next-sentence prediction (where the model determines if one sentence follows another in a given context).

Training and Capabilities:

BERT's bidirectional training allows it to grasp nuanced meanings and relationships between words, making it highly effective for tasks that require a deep understanding of context. It excels in question answering, named entity recognition, and sentiment analysis. For example, BERT can accurately identify entities like names and locations in text and answer questions based on context.

Applications:

BERT is widely used in applications such as search engines, where it improves query understanding and relevance, and in customer service chatbots, where it enhances intent recognition and response accuracy.

T5 (Text-to-Text Transfer Transformer)

Overview:

T5, developed by Google, takes a unified approach to various NLP tasks by framing them as text-to-text problems. This model treats all tasks—such as translation, summarization, and question answering—as transformations of text input into text output.

Architecture:

T5 uses a transformer encoder-decoder architecture, where both input and output are treated as text sequences. This allows it to handle a wide range of tasks within the same framework. The model is pre-trained on a diverse set of text-based tasks and fine-tuned for specific applications.

Training and Capabilities:

T5's flexibility enables it to perform a variety of tasks with high efficiency. It can generate summaries from long articles, translate text between languages, and create detailed responses to questions. Its ability to adapt to different tasks makes it a powerful tool for generating and transforming text.

Applications:

T5 is used in applications such as automated content generation, where it can create summaries of research papers or generate detailed explanations on complex topics. It is also used in multilingual translation systems, where it can handle translation tasks between multiple languages with high accuracy.

Natural Language Processing (NLP) Applications

Language models have revolutionized the field of NLP, enabling a wide range of applications that enhance how we interact with text. This section explores some prominent applications of text generation and their impact.

Text Generation

Content Creation:

Language models like GPT and T5 have transformed content creation by automating the generation of articles, blog posts, and marketing copy. These models can produce high-quality, coherent text tailored to specific topics or styles. For instance, GPT-3 can generate entire blog posts on various subjects, providing content creators with a valuable tool for speeding up the writing process.

Creative Writing:

In creative writing, language models assist authors in brainstorming ideas, drafting text, and exploring new narrative styles. They can generate poetry, stories, and scripts, offering inspiration and aiding in the creative process. For example, GPT-3 has been used to write short stories and poetry, showcasing its ability to mimic different writing styles.

Text Summarization

Extractive Summarization:

Extractive summarization involves selecting key sentences or phrases from a document to create a summary. Models like BERT can identify and extract the most important information, producing concise summaries that capture the essence of the original text. This approach is useful for generating summaries of news articles, research papers, and other lengthy documents.

Abstractive Summarization:

Abstractive summarization generates new sentences to convey the core message of a document. Models like T5 excel in this task by creating summaries that are more readable and coherent, often rewriting the content in a more concise form. This approach is valuable for summarizing complex information and creating digestible overviews.

Machine Translation

Language Translation:

Language models such as T5 and GPT can translate text between different languages, facilitating cross-linguistic communication and making content accessible to a global audience. These models leverage their understanding of context and semantics to produce accurate translations. For example, T5 has been used to translate text between multiple languages, providing high-quality translations for various applications.

Sentiment Analysis

Opinion Mining:

Language models analyze text to determine sentiment, such as positive, negative, or neutral opinions. This application is valuable for businesses monitoring customer feedback, social media, and product reviews. Models like BERT can accurately classify sentiment and provide insights into customer opinions and trends.

Chatbots and Conversational AI

Chatbots and conversational AI systems leverage language models to simulate human conversation, enhancing user interaction and providing automated responses. This section explores the functionality, applications, and challenges of these systems.

Functionality

Intent Recognition:

Chatbots use language models to understand user queries and identify the underlying intent. This allows them to provide relevant responses or take appropriate actions based on user input. For example, a customer service chatbot might use intent recognition to determine whether a user is asking for a product recommendation or reporting a problem.

Context Management:

Advanced conversational AI systems maintain context across interactions, enabling them to handle multi-turn conversations effectively. Models like GPT and BERT are used to remember previous exchanges and provide coherent responses, making conversations more natural and engaging.

Applications

Customer Support:

Chatbots powered by language models are increasingly used in customer service to handle inquiries, resolve issues, and provide information. They offer 24/7 support, reduce the need for human intervention, and improve response times. For instance, a chatbot might assist customers in tracking their orders, answering frequently asked questions, or troubleshooting technical problems.

Personal Assistants:

Conversational AI systems like virtual personal assistants (e.g., Siri, Alexa) use language models to perform tasks such as setting reminders, answering questions, and controlling smart home devices. These systems enhance user convenience and provide hands-free interaction with technology.

Challenges

Understanding Nuance:

Despite advances, chatbots may struggle with understanding complex queries or nuanced language. Language models must be continually improved to handle diverse user inputs and provide accurate responses. Addressing challenges like sarcasm, ambiguity, and cultural differences is essential for effective chatbot performance.

User Experience:

Ensuring a natural and engaging conversation experience is critical for effective chatbot deployment. Balancing automated responses with human-like interactions is essential for user satisfaction. Continuous testing and refinement are necessary to enhance the conversational abilities of chatbots.

Ethical Considerations in Text Generation

The deployment of advanced text generation models brings ethical considerations that must be addressed to ensure responsible use and mitigate potential risks.

Misinformation and Fake News

Content Authenticity:

The ability of language models to generate convincing text can be exploited to create and disseminate misinformation or fake news. Ensuring the authenticity of generated content is crucial for maintaining trust and credibility. Implementing content verification mechanisms and promoting media literacy can help combat misinformation.

Combating Misuse:

Strategies such as content moderation, detection systems, and user education are necessary to prevent the misuse of text generation technology for harmful purposes. Collaboration between technology providers, regulators, and the public is essential for addressing the challenges associated with misinformation.

Bias and Fairness

Model Bias:

Language models can inherit biases present in their training data, leading to biased or discriminatory outputs. Addressing these biases involves careful data curation, algorithmic fairness techniques, and ongoing evaluation. Techniques such as debiasing, bias detection, and inclusive data collection are important for reducing model bias.

Fair Representation:

Ensuring that language models represent diverse perspectives and avoid reinforcing stereotypes is essential for promoting fairness and inclusivity in generated content. Efforts to include diverse voices and perspectives in training data can help achieve more balanced and equitable outcomes.

Privacy and Security

Data Privacy:

The use of personal data for training language models raises privacy concerns. Implementing measures to protect user data and comply with privacy regulations is crucial for safeguarding sensitive information. Anonymization, data minimization, and secure data handling practices are important for protecting privacy.

Security Risks:

The generation of text with malicious intent, such as phishing or impersonation, poses security risks. Developing robust security protocols and monitoring systems can help mitigate these risks. Security measures such as content filtering, threat detection, and user authentication can enhance the safety of text generation systems.

Accountability and Transparency

Model Transparency:

Providing transparency about how language models are trained, evaluated, and deployed can enhance accountability and trust. Users should be informed about the capabilities and limitations of AI-generated text. Clear documentation, disclosure of training data sources, and explanations of model behavior can improve transparency.

Ethical Guidelines:

Establishing and adhering to ethical guidelines for the development and use of text generation models can guide responsible practices and prevent potential negative impacts. Engaging with stakeholders, including ethicists, policymakers, and the public, can help shape ethical standards and best practices.

Summary

Text generation has transformed the landscape of natural language processing, offering powerful tools for creating, understanding, and interacting with text. Language models like GPT, BERT, and T5 have advanced the capabilities of text generation, enabling a wide range of applications from content creation to conversational AI. However, the use of these models also raises ethical considerations that must be addressed to ensure responsible and fair deployment. By understanding the principles behind these models and their applications, as well as navigating the ethical landscape, we can harness the potential of text generation technology while mitigating its risks.

Key Takeaways

Language Models such as GPT, BERT, and T5 play a crucial role in text generation, each offering unique capabilities for understanding and creating text.

Applications of text generation include content creation, summarization, machine translation, and sentiment analysis, showcasing the versatility of language models in various domains.

Chatbots and Conversational AI leverage language models to simulate human conversation, enhancing customer service and user interaction with context-aware responses.

Ethical Considerations include addressing misinformation, bias, privacy, security, and accountability to ensure responsible use and prevent potential negative impacts of text generation technology.

Chapter 08: Image Generation

Introduction

Image generation is a powerful application of artificial intelligence (AI) that leverages sophisticated models and techniques to create and manipulate visual content. This chapter explores the key tools and techniques used in image generation, applications in creating art and logos, the impact of deepfakes, and the legal and ethical issues associated with these technologies.

Tools and Techniques: DALL-E, CLIP, StyleGAN

Advancements in AI have led to the development of several tools and techniques for image generation, each offering unique capabilities and applications. This section provides a detailed overview of DALL-E, CLIP, and StyleGAN.

DALL-E

Overview

DALL-E, developed by OpenAI, is a state-of-the-art model designed to generate images from textual descriptions. Its name reflects a combination of Salvador Dalí's surrealism and Pixar's WALL-E, highlighting its innovative approach to blending text and image generation.

Architecture

DALL-E utilizes a transformer-based architecture similar to GPT-3, but it is adapted for image generation. It encodes textual descriptions into a format that the model can use to generate corresponding images. DALL-E's model is trained on diverse datasets, allowing it to create images that align with a wide range of textual prompts.

Capabilities

DALL-E can generate highly creative and novel images from abstract or specific textual prompts. It can create images of objects, scenes, and even imaginative concepts that do not exist in reality, such as "a futuristic city on Mars" or "a cat wearing a space suit." This capability makes it valuable for creative industries, advertising, and visual content creation.

Applications

DALL-E is used in various domains, including product design, marketing, and entertainment. It enables rapid prototyping of visual ideas, generates unique visuals for campaigns, and assists in designing novel concepts based on user-defined descriptions.

CLIP (Contrastive Language-Image Pretraining)

Overview

CLIP, also developed by OpenAI, is designed to bridge the gap between textual and visual information. It understands and connects text and images by learning from a large dataset of image-text pairs.

Architecture

CLIP employs two separate encoders—one for text and one for images. Both encoders map their respective inputs into a shared embedding space, where similarity between text and images can be measured. This dual-encoder approach allows CLIP to evaluate how well images match textual descriptions and vice versa.

Capabilities

CLIP excels at zero-shot learning, meaning it can perform tasks without explicit training on those tasks. It can rank images based on their relevance to a text prompt, generate textual descriptions for images, and find images that match given descriptions. CLIP is useful for tasks like image search and content moderation.

Applications

CLIP is applied in image search engines, enabling users to find images based on textual queries. It also aids in generating textual descriptions of images, improving content accessibility, and enhancing AI-driven image analysis and classification systems.

StyleGAN

Overview:

StyleGAN, developed by NVIDIA, is a groundbreaking model known for its ability to generate high-quality, photorealistic images. It is particularly effective in creating images of human faces and other complex objects with detailed control over visual attributes.

Architecture:

StyleGAN uses a GAN framework with a style-based generator architecture. This design introduces style vectors that control different aspects of the generated images, such as facial expressions, hairstyles, and backgrounds. The model's discriminator evaluates the realism of the images produced by the generator.

Capabilities:

StyleGAN can produce highly realistic images by manipulating the style vectors. For instance, it can generate diverse and lifelike human faces with varying attributes, such as age, gender, and facial expressions. The model's ability to control style parameters allows for precise adjustments in generated images.

Applications:

StyleGAN is used in creating realistic avatars, virtual models, and artistic visuals. It is valuable in industries such as fashion and entertainment for designing virtual characters and visual content. Additionally, StyleGAN has applications in data augmentation and research in generative art.

Creating Art, Logos, and Visual Content

AI tools have transformed the creation of art, logos, and other visual content by offering new methods for generating and manipulating images. This section explores how these tools are utilized in various creative processes.

Art Creation

Generative Art:

AI tools like DALL-E and StyleGAN are used to create generative art, where AI generates unique visual pieces based on specified parameters or random inputs. Generative art explores new artistic styles and visual concepts, enabling artists to produce novel and diverse artworks.

Collaborative Art:

AI can collaborate with human artists to enhance the creative process. Artists may use AI-generated images as starting points or inspiration for their work. AI tools can generate variations of initial sketches or ideas, providing artists with new perspectives and possibilities.

Logo Design

Custom Logos:

Tools like DALL-E can generate logos based on textual descriptions, offering a quick and efficient way to explore different design options. For example, a business might input a description like "a minimalist logo with a green leaf," and DALL-E generates several logo concepts to choose from.

Design Variations:

AI tools can create variations of existing logos by adjusting design elements such as colors, fonts, and shapes. This capability allows businesses to explore different styles and formats, helping them find the best design for their brand.

Visual Content for Marketing

Advertising Graphics:

AI-generated images are used in marketing to create eye-catching visuals tailored to specific campaigns. DALL-E and CLIP can generate images that align with marketing messages, helping brands produce compelling and relevant content for their target audiences.

Social Media Content:

AI tools can generate engaging social media visuals, including banners, infographics, and promotional graphics. By leveraging models like StyleGAN, businesses can create high-quality visuals that capture attention and enhance their online presence.

Deepfakes: Creation and Detection

Deepfakes represent a significant advancement in image and video manipulation, driven by AI technologies. This section explores how deepfakes are created, detected, and the associated challenges.

Creation of Deepfakes

Technology:

Deepfakes are created using techniques such as GANs and autoencoders. These models learn to replicate facial features, expressions, and voice patterns by training on large datasets of images or videos of individuals. The resulting synthetic content can closely mimic real people, leading to highly realistic manipulations.

Applications:

While deepfakes have legitimate uses in entertainment and special effects, they also pose risks when used maliciously. They can create misleading or harmful content, such as fake news videos or fraudulent recordings, raising concerns about misinformation and security.

Detection of Deepfakes

Techniques:

Detecting deepfakes involves analyzing visual and audio cues for anomalies that may indicate manipulation. Techniques include using deep learning models trained to recognize deepfake artifacts, examining inconsistencies in facial expressions or voice patterns, and applying forensic analysis tools.

Challenges:

As deepfake technology advances, detecting manipulated content becomes more challenging. Researchers are developing new methods to improve detection accuracy, including multi-modal approaches that combine visual, audio, and contextual information.

Legal and Ethical Issues in Image Generation

The rapid development of image generation technologies has brought about significant legal and ethical considerations. This section addresses these issues and their implications.

Copyright and Intellectual Property

Ownership:

The creation of AI-generated images raises questions about copyright ownership. Determining who owns the rights to AI-generated content—whether it's the human creator, the AI developer, or the user—requires clarity in legal frameworks. Copyright laws may need to evolve to address these new challenges.

Usage Rights:

Ensuring that AI-generated images are used in accordance with licensing agreements and usage rights is essential. Users must adhere to the terms specified by AI tool creators and avoid infringing on the intellectual property rights of others.

Misuse and Harmful Content

Misleading Information:

The ability to create realistic images and videos can be misused to generate misleading or harmful content. Addressing this issue involves implementing safeguards to prevent the creation and distribution of fake or malicious content and promoting responsible use of image generation technology.

Privacy Concerns:

The use of AI to generate images of individuals, especially without their consent, raises privacy concerns. Ensuring that image generation tools are used in compliance with privacy regulations and respecting individuals' rights to control their likeness is crucial for protecting personal privacy.

Ethical Considerations

Transparency:

Providing transparency about how image generation models are trained and used helps build trust and accountability. Users should be informed about the capabilities and limitations of these models, as well as the potential ethical implications of their use.

Bias and Fairness:

Addressing biases in image generation models is important for ensuring fair and equitable outcomes. Efforts should be made to identify and mitigate biases in training data and model outputs to prevent the reinforcement of stereotypes or discrimination.

Summary

Image generation technologies have transformed the creation and manipulation of visual content, offering powerful tools for artists, designers, and content creators. Tools like DALL-E, CLIP, and StyleGAN enable the generation of diverse and high-quality images, enhancing creativity and efficiency in various applications. However, the rise of deepfakes and associated legal and ethical issues highlight the need for responsible use and regulatory frameworks. By understanding these technologies and their implications, we can harness their potential while addressing the challenges and ensuring ethical practices.

Key Takeaways

Advanced Tools: DALL-E, CLIP, and StyleGAN are key tools in image generation, each offering unique capabilities for creating and manipulating visual content. They enable diverse applications from art creation to logo design and marketing.

Creative Potential: AI tools enhance creativity by generating novel visual content, providing new opportunities for art, design, and advertising.

Deepfake Risks: The creation and detection of deepfakes highlight the need for vigilance in managing the risks associated with manipulated content. Effective detection methods and security measures are essential.

Legal and Ethical Challenges: Addressing copyright, misuse, privacy, and bias concerns is crucial for the responsible use of image generation technologies. Transparent practices and ethical guidelines help navigate these challenges and promote fair use.

Chapter 09: Music and Audio Generation

Introduction

Music and audio generation through artificial intelligence (AI) have opened new avenues for creativity, enabling innovative approaches to composing music, generating sound effects, and creating immersive audio experiences. This chapter delves into how AI is transforming the world of music and audio, explores tools and models used in audio generation, and examines the diverse applications of these technologies in various industries.

AI in Music Composition

AI has significantly impacted music composition by offering new methods and tools that enhance and expand the creative process. This section explores how AI contributes to music composition, the techniques used, and the implications for composers and the music industry.

Generative Models for Music

Overview:

Generative models are designed to produce new musical compositions by learning patterns from existing musical data. These models analyze vast amounts of music to understand the underlying structures, styles, and elements of various genres. They can then generate original music that adheres to these learned patterns.

Techniques:

- **Recurrent Neural Networks (RNNs):** RNNs, including Long Short-Term Memory (LSTM) networks, are effective in generating sequences of musical notes, chords, or rhythms. They are particularly suited for tasks that involve temporal dependencies, such as composing melodies or harmonies.
- **Transformers:** Transformers, known for their attention mechanisms, have been adapted for music composition. They model long-range dependencies and generate complex musical structures by attending to different parts of the musical sequence simultaneously.
- **Variational Autoencoders (VAEs):** VAEs learn probabilistic representations of music by encoding musical data into a latent space and decoding it to generate new samples. This approach allows for the creation of diverse and novel musical content by sampling from the latent space.

Interactive Composition Tools

AI-Assisted Composing:

AI-assisted composing tools help musicians by providing suggestions for melodies, harmonies, or rhythmic patterns. These tools can generate variations of musical themes or complete compositions based on user input, allowing composers to explore new ideas and enhance their creative workflow.

Real-Time Composition:

AI systems that support real-time composition can generate music dynamically based on live inputs, such as a musician's performance or user interactions. These systems can create accompanying music for live performances or generate music in interactive applications, adapting to the user's actions or preferences.

Music Style Transfer

Overview:

Music style transfer involves applying the stylistic elements of one musical piece to another, allowing for the transformation of compositions while preserving their original content. This technique uses AI to transfer characteristics such as rhythms, harmonies, and timbres between different pieces of music.

Applications:

Music style transfer can create unique variations of existing compositions, blend different musical styles, or reimagine classical works in contemporary genres. It offers new creative possibilities and allows composers to experiment with different styles and genres.

Tools and Models for Audio Generation

Various tools and models have been developed to generate audio content, ranging from music and sound effects to speech and environmental sounds. This section covers some of the key tools and models used in audio generation and their capabilities.

Music Generation Tools

OpenAI MuseNet:

MuseNet is a deep learning model developed by OpenAI that can generate music across a wide range of genres and styles. It leverages a transformer-based architecture to produce compositions with coherent melodies, harmonies, and rhythms. MuseNet can create complex musical pieces, including multi-instrumental arrangements, by learning from diverse musical datasets.

AIVA (Artificial Intelligence Virtual Artist):

AIVA is an AI composer designed to create original music compositions tailored to specific requirements, such as mood, style, or instrumentation. AIVA uses a combination of deep learning techniques and human input to generate music that meets the needs of various applications, including film scores, commercials, and personal projects.

Audio Generation Models

WaveNet:

Developed by DeepMind, WaveNet is a generative model for producing high-quality audio waveforms. It uses a deep convolutional architecture to generate audio samples one step at a time, resulting in realistic and natural-sounding speech and music. WaveNet has been applied to text-to-speech synthesis and audio generation tasks.

SampleRNN:

SampleRNN is a hierarchical generative model that generates audio sequences by modeling dependencies at different time scales. It is used to create diverse audio samples, including music and speech, by learning from large datasets of audio recordings. SampleRNN can capture complex patterns in audio data and produce high-quality results.

Speech Synthesis and Voice Generation

Tacotron:

Tacotron is a sequence-to-sequence model for speech synthesis that generates natural-sounding speech from textual input. It combines a sequence-to-sequence framework with a neural vocoder to produce high-quality synthetic speech that closely resembles human speech.

WaveGlow:

sequences or create new content by learning from existing frames. This is useful for tasks such as object removal or scene completion.

Applications in Film, Animation, and Virtual Reality

AI-driven video and animation technologies have widespread applications across various media industries, revolutionizing the way content is created and experienced.

Film Production

Visual Effects (VFX):

AI enhances VFX in films by generating realistic CGI, adding special effects, and enhancing visual elements. AI techniques can create complex visual effects like explosions, weather changes, and fantastical creatures with high realism.

Scene Generation:

AI can generate virtual environments and backgrounds for films. Techniques such as video-to-video translation and neural rendering enable filmmakers to create immersive and visually stunning scenes without extensive manual effort.

Animation

Automated Animation:

AI tools automate parts of the animation process, such as generating in-between frames or creating character animations from motion capture data. This reduces manual effort and accelerates production timelines, making animation more efficient and cost-effective.

Style Transfer:

AI-driven style transfer techniques can apply various artistic styles to animated content, transforming animations into different visual aesthetics or mimicking the styles of renowned artists. This opens up creative possibilities for animators and studios.

Virtual Reality (VR)

Immersive Content Creation:

AI facilitates the creation of immersive VR experiences by generating realistic 3D environments and animations. Techniques like neural rendering and video synthesis allow for dynamic and interactive VR content that enhances user immersion.

Real-Time Interaction:

AI-driven video generation enables real-time interaction and adaptation within VR environments. This includes generating responsive animations and adapting virtual characters' behaviors based on user inputs, creating more engaging and interactive experiences.

Challenges and Future Directions

Despite the advancements, there are challenges and considerations in the field of video and animation generation. Addressing these challenges is crucial for advancing the technology and ensuring its responsible use.

Challenges

Data Quality and Diversity:

High-quality and diverse training data are essential for generating realistic video content. Limited availability of such data can impact the quality and versatility of generated videos. Collecting and curating diverse datasets is a significant challenge.

Computational Resources:

Video synthesis and rendering require substantial computational resources, including powerful GPUs and large-scale processing capabilities. This can be a barrier to accessing advanced techniques and technologies, particularly for smaller studios or individuals.

Ethical Concerns:

The ability to generate realistic videos raises ethical concerns related to misinformation, deepfakes, and privacy. Addressing potential misuse and ensuring responsible use of video generation technologies are critical to mitigating these concerns.

Future Directions

Improved Models:

Future advancements will focus on enhancing the quality, realism, and efficiency of video generation techniques. Developing models that can generate high-resolution videos with improved temporal coherence and visual fidelity is a key area of research.

Interactive and Personalized Content:

AI-driven video generation will increasingly support interactive and personalized content. This includes creating adaptive video experiences that respond to user preferences and interactions, leading to more engaging and tailored content.

Integration with Augmented Reality (AR):

Integrating video generation technologies with AR will enable the creation of immersive experiences that blend virtual and real-world elements. This integration has potential applications in entertainment, education, marketing, and more.

Summary

AI-driven video and animation generation technologies have significantly transformed the media and entertainment industries. From advanced synthesis techniques to applications in film, animation, and VR, AI has expanded the creative possibilities for video production and manipulation. While challenges remain, ongoing advancements promise to enhance the quality, realism, and interactivity of video content, shaping the future of media and entertainment.

Key Takeaways

Advanced Techniques: AI-driven techniques like GANs, VAEs, and neural rendering have revolutionized video synthesis, enabling the creation of high-quality and realistic video content.

Diverse Applications: AI technologies are applied across film, animation, and VR, enhancing production processes and enabling new forms of creative expression.

Challenges and Considerations: Data quality, computational resources, and ethical concerns are key challenges in video generation. Addressing these challenges is essential for the responsible and effective use of AI technologies.

Future Prospects: Future developments in AI video generation will focus on improving model capabilities, supporting interactive and personalized content, and integrating with emerging technologies like AR, opening new possibilities for media and entertainment.

Chapter 11: Generative AI in Healthcare

Introduction

Generative AI is redefining the landscape of healthcare, offering innovative solutions that streamline drug discovery, enhance medical imaging, and personalize treatment plans. This chapter delves into the applications of generative AI across various healthcare domains, exploring how these technologies are revolutionizing patient care and medical research.

Drug Discovery and Development

Drug discovery and development are among the most complex and costly phases in bringing new treatments to market. Generative AI offers transformative solutions by optimizing various aspects of drug development.

1. Accelerating Drug Discovery

Molecular Design and Optimization:

- **Generative Models for Molecular Design:** AI models like GANs and VAEs can generate novel molecular structures by learning from existing data. These models predict which molecular configurations might be effective against specific targets.

- **Drug-like Property Prediction:** Generative AI can predict the properties of newly designed molecules, such as solubility and toxicity, speeding up the selection of viable drug candidates.

Automated High-Throughput Screening:

- **Virtual Screening:** AI-driven virtual screening allows researchers to test millions of compounds in silico, reducing the need for physical testing and accelerating the identification of potential drug candidates.
- **Simulation of Drug Interactions:** AI models simulate interactions between drugs and biological targets, predicting potential efficacy and adverse effects.

2. Enhancing Drug Repurposing

Repurposing Existing Drugs:

- **Novel Applications:** Generative AI can identify new therapeutic uses for existing drugs by analyzing patterns in biological and chemical data, providing new treatment options for diseases with limited therapies.
- **Target Identification:** AI models can uncover new drug targets by analyzing large datasets of genomic and proteomic information.

3. Optimizing Clinical Trials

Patient Selection and Stratification:

- **Precision Recruitment:** AI algorithms analyze patient data to identify individuals who meet specific criteria for clinical trials, ensuring that trials are conducted on the most appropriate candidates.
- **Predictive Analytics for Outcomes:** Generative models can predict the outcomes of clinical trials based on historical data, helping in designing more effective trials and minimizing risks.

Adaptive Trial Designs:

- **Real-Time Adjustments:** AI can monitor ongoing trials and suggest adjustments to protocols based on real-time data, improving the efficiency and success rate of clinical trials.

Medical Imaging and Diagnostics

Generative AI is significantly enhancing the quality and efficiency of medical imaging and diagnostics, offering new capabilities in image enhancement, analysis, and disease detection.

1. Image Enhancement

Resolution and Quality Improvement:

- **Super-Resolution Techniques:** AI models enhance the resolution of medical images, such as MRI and CT scans, improving detail and accuracy in diagnostics.
- **Noise Reduction:** Generative AI algorithms reduce noise and artifacts in imaging data, enhancing the clarity and diagnostic value of medical images.

Image Reconstruction:

- **Advanced Reconstruction Methods:** AI-driven reconstruction techniques improve the quality of images obtained from limited data or suboptimal imaging conditions, leading to more accurate diagnoses.

2. Automated Image Analysis

Segmentation and Localization:

- **Automated Segmentation:** AI models automatically segment images to identify and outline regions of interest, such as tumors or organs, facilitating more accurate and faster analysis.

- **Feature Extraction:** Generative AI extracts and quantifies features from medical images, such as lesion size and shape, aiding in diagnosis and treatment planning.

Disease Detection and Classification:

- **Anomaly Detection:** AI models identify anomalies in medical images, such as early-stage tumors or irregularities, providing early warnings for potential diseases.
- **Disease Classification:** Generative AI classifies medical images into different disease categories, helping radiologists make more accurate diagnoses and treatment decisions.

3. Enhancing Diagnostic Accuracy

Integration with Electronic Health Records (EHRs):

- **Data Fusion:** AI integrates imaging data with patient EHRs to provide a comprehensive view of the patient's health, improving diagnostic accuracy and treatment planning.
- **Decision Support Systems:** AI-powered decision support systems assist healthcare professionals in interpreting complex imaging data and making informed decisions.

Personalized Treatment Plans

Generative AI contributes to personalized medicine by analyzing individual patient data to create customized treatment plans that enhance efficacy and reduce adverse effects.

1. Genomic Data Analysis

Variant Interpretation and Analysis:

- **Identifying Genetic Variants:** AI models analyze genomic data to identify genetic variants associated with diseases, providing insights into individual risk profiles and potential treatment options.

- **Predictive Modeling for Drug Response:** Generative AI predicts how different genetic profiles will respond to various treatments, allowing for more personalized and effective therapies.

Integration of Multi-Omics Data:

- **Holistic View:** AI integrates genomic, transcriptomic, proteomic, and metabolomic data to provide a comprehensive view of an individual's health, aiding in personalized treatment planning.
- **Disease Mechanism Understanding:** AI models help in understanding the underlying mechanisms of diseases by analyzing multi-omics data, leading to the development of targeted therapies.

2. Optimizing Treatment Regimens

Personalized Drug Selection:

- **AI-Driven Recommendations:** AI algorithms recommend personalized drug regimens based on individual patient data, improving treatment outcomes and minimizing side effects.
- **Dosage Optimization:** Generative AI models suggest optimal drug dosages tailored to individual patient characteristics, enhancing treatment safety and efficacy.

Behavioral and Lifestyle Adjustments:

- **Customized Recommendations:** AI analyzes lifestyle data to provide personalized recommendations for diet, exercise, and other behavioral factors that impact health.
- **Predictive Analytics for Health Risks:** AI models predict potential health risks based on lifestyle and genetic data, enabling proactive interventions and preventive measures.

Summary

Generative AI is reshaping the healthcare landscape by advancing drug discovery, enhancing medical imaging and diagnostics, and enabling personalized treatment plans. These technologies offer innovative solutions that streamline processes, improve patient outcomes, and drive progress in medical research. As AI continues to evolve, its potential to revolutionize healthcare and enhance the quality of patient care will expand, offering new possibilities for personalized medicine and efficient healthcare delivery.

Key Takeaways

Drug Discovery and Development: Generative AI accelerates drug discovery by designing novel compounds, predicting drug interactions, and optimizing clinical trials, reducing time and costs in drug development.

Medical Imaging and Diagnostics: AI enhances medical imaging through super-resolution and noise reduction, automates image analysis with segmentation and feature extraction, and improves disease detection and classification.

Personalized Treatment Plans: AI contributes to personalized medicine by analyzing genomic data, optimizing treatment regimens, and providing lifestyle recommendations based on individual patient profiles.

Future Prospects: Continued advancements in generative AI will further transform healthcare, leading to more precise diagnostics, effective treatments, and personalized care strategies.

Part IV: Advanced Topics in Generative AI

Chapter 12: Ethical and Social Implications

Introduction

Generative AI technologies, such as those used for creating images, text, and audio, are transforming various fields and introducing new capabilities and efficiencies. However, their rapid development and deployment bring complex ethical and social implications that must be addressed to ensure their responsible and equitable use. This chapter delves into the key ethical and social concerns related to AI, focusing on AI bias and fairness, ownership and intellectual property, and the broader role of AI in society.

AI Bias and Fairness

AI systems, including generative models, often reflect and amplify the biases present in their training data, which can lead to unfair outcomes and perpetuate societal inequalities. Addressing these biases is crucial for creating equitable and trustworthy AI technologies.

1. Sources of AI Bias

Training Data Bias:

- **Historical Bias:** AI systems trained on historical data may inherit and perpetuate existing societal biases. For example, if a

model is trained on data with historical gender or racial biases, it can produce biased results that reinforce these disparities.
- **Sampling Bias:** Biases can also arise from unrepresentative data samples. For instance, if a dataset predominantly features data from one demographic group, the model may perform poorly for individuals outside this group.

Algorithmic Bias:

- **Model Design:** The design of machine learning algorithms can introduce bias. For example, certain algorithms may make decisions that disproportionately impact specific groups if not carefully calibrated.
- **Feature Selection:** The choice of features used in training can also lead to bias. If certain features encode prejudiced information, the model's predictions can become biased.

2. Addressing AI Bias

Diverse and Representative Data:

- **Inclusive Data Collection:** To mitigate biases, it's essential to collect diverse and representative datasets. This includes ensuring that data reflects various demographics, contexts, and conditions.
- **Bias Audits:** Conducting regular audits of AI systems to identify and address biases is crucial. Techniques such as fairness-aware modeling and adversarial debiasing can help mitigate bias in training data and model outputs.

Ethical Guidelines and Frameworks:

- **Fairness Frameworks:** Implementing fairness frameworks helps guide the development of AI systems to ensure they are designed and evaluated with fairness in mind. These frameworks provide principles for assessing and addressing biases.

- **Transparency and Accountability:** Promoting transparency in AI decision-making processes and holding developers accountable for biased outcomes fosters trust and ensures ethical AI practices.

Ownership and Intellectual Property

The rise of generative AI raises complex questions about ownership and intellectual property (IP). Determining who owns AI-generated content and addressing its implications for creativity and innovation are critical issues.

1. Ownership of AI-Generated Content

Authorship and Attribution:

- **AI as an Author:** The question of authorship for AI-generated content—such as art, music, or literature—poses challenges. Traditional IP laws are designed for human creators, and applying these principles to AI-generated works is a subject of ongoing debate.
- **Attribution Issues:** When AI generates content based on existing works, issues of attribution and credit arise. For example, if an AI model creates art inspired by existing styles, determining the original creator's credit becomes complex.

Legal Frameworks:

- **Current IP Laws:** Existing IP laws may not fully address the nuances of AI-generated content. There is ongoing debate about whether AI should be recognized as a legal entity with IP rights or if the rights should belong to the developers or users of the AI.
- **Proposed Reforms:** New legal frameworks and reforms are being proposed to address ownership and protection of AI-generated works. These reforms aim to balance the interests of AI developers, users, and human creators, ensuring fair and clear IP rights.

2. Ethical Implications of AI-Generated Content

Creativity and Innovation:

- **Impact on Human Creativity:** AI's ability to generate content raises questions about its impact on human creativity. While AI can produce impressive works, it is important to consider how this affects the value and originality of human-created content.
- **Monetization and Fair Compensation:** Ensuring fair compensation for human creators and developers involved in AI-generated works is important. Fair compensation mechanisms should be established to balance the interests of all parties involved.

Cultural and Social Impact:

- **Cultural Appropriation:** AI-generated content that incorporates cultural elements may raise concerns about cultural appropriation. Respecting intellectual and cultural heritage while generating new content is essential.
- **Misuse of AI-Generated Works:** The potential misuse of AI-generated content, such as creating deepfakes or deceptive media, poses significant ethical concerns. Safeguards and regulations are necessary to prevent malicious uses and ensure responsible AI practices.

The Role of AI in Society: Risks and Rewards

AI's integration into various aspects of society offers substantial benefits but also presents challenges. Understanding the risks and rewards associated with AI deployment is crucial for maximizing its positive impact while minimizing potential harm.

1. Risks Associated with AI

Privacy Concerns:

- **Data Collection and Surveillance:** The use of AI often involves the collection and analysis of vast amounts of personal data, raising concerns about privacy and surveillance. Implementing robust data protection measures is critical for safeguarding individuals' privacy.
- **Data Security:** Ensuring the security of AI systems and the data they handle is crucial. This includes protecting against unauthorized access, breaches, and misuse of sensitive information.

Job Displacement:

- **Automation Impact:** AI's capacity to automate tasks may lead to job displacement and shifts in the labor market. Developing policies for workforce transition, reskilling, and support for affected workers is important to address these impacts.
- **Economic Inequality:** The benefits of AI may not be evenly distributed, potentially exacerbating economic inequality. Ensuring equitable access to AI technologies and opportunities can help mitigate disparities.

Ethical Decision-Making:

- **Moral and Ethical Dilemmas:** AI systems may face complex moral and ethical dilemmas, such as making decisions in life-critical situations. Developing ethical decision-making frameworks and accountability mechanisms is essential for addressing these challenges.

2. Rewards and Opportunities

Enhanced Efficiency and Productivity:

- **Operational Efficiency:** AI can significantly enhance efficiency and productivity across various sectors, including healthcare, finance, and manufacturing. Leveraging AI technologies can lead to cost savings, improved processes, and better outcomes.
- **Innovation and Advancement:** AI drives innovation by enabling new applications and solutions that were previously unimaginable. Continued AI development offers opportunities for breakthrough advancements and discoveries.

Improved Quality of Life:

- **Personalization:** AI enables personalized experiences and solutions, such as tailored healthcare treatments, customized recommendations, and enhanced user experiences. These advancements can lead to improved quality of life and better outcomes for individuals.
- **Problem Solving:** AI has the potential to address complex global challenges, such as climate change, disease prevention, and disaster response. Harnessing AI for social good can lead to significant positive impacts.

Summary

The integration of generative AI technologies into various sectors brings both opportunities and challenges. Addressing the ethical and social implications of AI—such as bias and fairness, ownership and intellectual property, and its broader role in society—is essential for ensuring responsible and equitable AI development. By fostering ethical practices, promoting transparency, and balancing risks with rewards, society can harness the full potential of AI while mitigating negative impacts and advancing towards a more equitable and innovative future.

Key Takeaways

AI Bias and Fairness: AI systems can inherit and amplify biases present in training data. Mitigating bias requires diverse data, fairness frameworks, and transparency to ensure equitable outcomes and foster trust in AI technologies.

Ownership and Intellectual Property: Determining ownership of AI-generated content poses challenges for existing IP laws. Legal reforms and ethical considerations are needed to address authorship, attribution, and fair compensation.

The Role of AI in Society: AI offers significant benefits, including enhanced efficiency and improved quality of life, but also presents risks such as privacy concerns, job displacement, and ethical dilemmas. Balancing these factors is crucial for responsible AI deployment and maximizing its positive impact.

Chapter 13: Challenges in Generative AI

Introduction

Generative AI has revolutionized various fields by enabling the creation of novel content. However, its advancement comes with a set of significant challenges that need to be addressed to fully harness its potential and ensure responsible usage. This chapter delves deeper into the key challenges in generative AI, including quality control and content coherence, computational requirements, managing and mitigating ethical concerns, and other emerging issues.

Quality Control and Content Coherence

Content Accuracy and Reliability

Ensuring Accuracy:

Ensuring the accuracy of generated content is crucial, especially in applications where factual correctness is paramount, such as in medical diagnostics or new generation. Techniques such as fact-checking algorithms and validation against trusted data sources can help maintain accuracy.

Model Robustness:

Developing models that are robust to diverse and complex inputs helps improve reliability. This includes training on diverse datasets and incorporating techniques to handle edge cases and unexpected inputs.

Consistency and Relevance

Maintaining Contextual Consistency:

For tasks such as narrative generation, ensuring that content remains contextually consistent over long passages is a challenge. Techniques like memory networks and attention mechanisms are employed to manage long-term dependencies and maintain coherence.

Relevance to Prompts:

Ensuring that generated content is relevant to the input prompts or context is essential. Techniques like prompt engineering and dynamic attention can enhance the model's ability to generate contextually appropriate responses.

Evaluation Metrics and Methods

Developing New Metrics:

Traditional evaluation metrics may not fully capture the quality of generative content. Developing new metrics tailored to specific generative tasks, such as human-centric evaluations or task-specific benchmarks, is necessary.

User Feedback and Iterative Improvement:

Incorporating user feedback and iterative refinement processes helps enhance content quality. Continuous learning from user interactions and feedback loops can improve model performance and content relevance.

Computational Requirements

Hardware and Infrastructure

High-Performance Computing:

Training and deploying large generative models require significant computational power, including high-performance GPUs or TPUs. Advancements in hardware, such as more efficient processors and accelerators, can help meet these demands.

Cloud Computing Solutions:

Leveraging cloud computing resources for scalable training and deployment offers flexibility and reduces the need for extensive on-premises infrastructure. Cloud providers offer specialized services and infrastructure optimized for AI workloads.

Resource Efficiency and Optimization

Model Optimization Techniques:

Techniques such as model pruning, quantization, and knowledge distillation can reduce the computational and memory requirements of generative models while maintaining performance. Efficient model architectures also play a role in reducing resource consumption.

Energy Consumption:

Managing energy consumption is crucial, especially given the large-scale computations involved. Implementing energy-efficient algorithms and optimizing training processes can help mitigate environmental impacts.

Cost Management

Training Costs:

The financial costs associated with training large generative models can be substantial. Budgeting for hardware, cloud services, and operational expenses is necessary to manage costs effectively.

Operational Costs:

Ongoing costs for maintaining and running generative models in production include infrastructure, data storage, and energy usage. Cost-effective strategies and cloud solutions can help manage these expenses.

Managing and Mitigating Ethical Concerns

Preventing Misuse

Deepfakes and Fake Media:

The creation of deepfakes and other deceptive content poses significant ethical concerns. Developing detection algorithms and implementing verification systems are essential for combating misuse. Additionally, raising awareness and providing training on the ethical use of AI technologies can help prevent abuse.

Regulation and Policy:

Establishing regulations and policies for the responsible use of generative AI can help prevent misuse. Policies should include guidelines for transparency, accountability, and the ethical use of AI-generated content.

Addressing Bias and Fairness

Bias Detection and Mitigation:

Generative models can inadvertently perpetuate biases present in training data. Implementing techniques for bias detection and mitigation, such as fairness-aware algorithms and diverse training datasets, helps address these issues.

Inclusive Design Practices:

Designing generative models with inclusivity in mind ensures that they serve diverse populations and avoid discriminatory outcomes. This includes considering various demographic factors and promoting fair representation in generated content.

Transparency and Accountability

Model Transparency:

Providing transparency into the workings of generative models helps build trust and accountability. This includes explaining the model's decision-making processes, training data, and potential limitations.

Accountability Mechanisms:

Establishing accountability mechanisms for the development and deployment of generative AI ensures responsible practices. This includes implementing oversight, audits, and review processes to address ethical concerns and ensure adherence to guidelines.

Privacy and Data Security

Data Privacy:

Ensuring the privacy of sensitive data used in training generative models is crucial. Techniques such as data anonymization and differential privacy can help protect individual privacy while using large datasets.

Security Measures:

Implementing robust security measures to protect AI models and data from unauthorized access and potential attacks is essential for maintaining trust and integrity.

Societal and Long-Term Implications

Impact on Employment and Labor Markets

Job Displacement:

The widespread adoption of generative AI can impact job markets by automating tasks traditionally performed by humans. Addressing potential job displacement through reskilling programs and support for affected workers is necessary.

New Opportunities:

Generative AI also creates new opportunities in fields such as AI research, content creation, and technology development. Fostering innovation and exploring new career paths can help balance the impact on employment.

Social and Cultural Impact

Influence on Media and Culture:

Generative AI technologies influence media and cultural production, potentially altering how content is created and consumed. Understanding and managing these cultural shifts is important for ensuring positive outcomes.

Public Perception and Trust:

Building public trust in generative AI involves transparent practices, ethical considerations, and responsible use. Engaging with the public and addressing concerns can help foster a positive perception of AI technologies.

Future Research and Development

Advancing AI Research:

Continued research into improving generative AI models, addressing limitations, and exploring new applications is essential for advancing the field. Collaboration between academia, industry, and policymakers can drive innovation and progress.

Exploring New Applications:

Investigating new and emerging applications of generative AI can uncover novel use cases and opportunities. Staying abreast of technological advancements and exploring their potential impacts can shape the future of AI.

Summary

Addressing the challenges in generative AI requires a multifaceted approach, encompassing quality control, computational efficiency, ethical considerations, and societal impacts. By developing effective strategies and solutions for these challenges, stakeholders can maximize the benefits of generative AI while mitigating risks. Ensuring that generative AI technologies are used responsibly and ethically is crucial for harnessing their potential and contributing positively to society.

Key Takeaways

> **Quality Control and Content Coherence:** Ensuring the accuracy, consistency, and relevance of generated content is critical. Advanced techniques and human oversight play essential roles in maintaining high standards.
>
> **Computational Requirements:** Generative AI models demand significant computational resources, including processing power and storage. Efficient optimization and leveraging advanced hardware are key to managing these requirements.

Managing Ethical Concerns: Addressing ethical challenges, such as preventing misuse, ensuring fairness, and considering long-term implications, is crucial for responsible AI development. Transparency, accountability, and inclusivity are vital for fostering ethical practices.

Societal and Long-Term Implications: The impact of generative AI on employment, culture, and society requires careful consideration. Balancing innovation with ethical considerations and exploring new opportunities can help navigate the evolving landscape of AI.

Chapter 14: Integrating Generative AI with Other Technologies

Introduction

The convergence of generative AI with other advanced technologies offers transformative possibilities, enhancing functionality and unlocking new applications across diverse fields. This chapter delves into the integration of generative AI with the Internet of Things (IoT), cloud computing, and explores cross-disciplinary innovations, examining how these synergies drive technological advancements and shape future developments.

AI and IoT: Smart Content Creation

Enhancing IoT Devices with Generative AI

Predictive Analytics and Modeling:

Generative AI can improve the accuracy of predictive analytics in IoT applications. By generating synthetic data, AI models can simulate various scenarios and predict outcomes more accurately, aiding in decision-making processes for smart cities, agriculture, and industrial operations.

Real-Time Data Generation:

IoT devices equipped with generative AI can create real-time data streams for dynamic applications, such as autonomous vehicles or smart grids. This capability supports continuous monitoring and adaptive responses to changing conditions.

Personalized User Experiences

Adaptive User Interfaces:

Generative AI can be used to develop adaptive user interfaces for IoT devices, offering personalized interactions based on user behavior and preferences. For example, smart thermostats can learn from user patterns to generate optimal heating and cooling schedules.

Intelligent Recommendations:

Leveraging data from IoT sensors, generative AI can provide personalized recommendations across various domains, including smart home systems, healthcare wearables, and fitness trackers, enhancing user experience and engagement.

Integration Challenges and Solutions

Data Privacy and Security:

Integrating generative AI with IoT requires robust data protection measures. Techniques such as federated learning, which keeps data decentralized while training models, can help mitigate privacy concerns.

Interoperability and Standardization:

Achieving seamless integration involves addressing interoperability issues between diverse IoT devices and AI systems. Establishing common standards and protocols can facilitate better communication and data exchange.

AI in Cloud Computing

Scalability and Resource Management

- **Elastic Compute Resources:** Cloud platforms provide elastic compute resources that scale according to the demands of generative AI tasks. This scalability is crucial for handling the intensive processing requirements of training large models and generating high-quality outputs.
- **Storage Solutions:** Cloud storage solutions offer the capacity to manage large datasets necessary for generative AI applications. Advanced storage technologies, such as distributed file systems and object storage, ensure efficient data management and retrieval.

Collaborative Development and Deployment

- **Integrated Development Environments:** Cloud platforms provide integrated development environments (IDEs) and tools that support collaborative development of generative AI models. These environments streamline code sharing, version control, and collaborative experimentation.
- **CI/CD Pipelines for AI Models:** Continuous integration and continuous deployment (CI/CD) pipelines in the cloud facilitate the iterative development and deployment of AI models. This approach ensures that updates are quickly integrated and deployed, enhancing the model's performance and reliability.

Enhanced AI Services and Tools

- **Managed AI Services:** Cloud providers offer managed AI services that simplify the deployment and management of generative models. These services include pre-trained models, automated machine learning (AutoML) tools, and advanced analytics capabilities.
- **Big Data Analytics:** Cloud-based big data analytics tools complement generative AI by providing advanced analytics and visualization capabilities. These tools enable deeper insights

into data generated by AI models and support data-driven decision-making.

Cross-Disciplinary Applications and Innovations

Integrating AI with Healthcare Technologies

Drug Discovery and Development:

Generative AI models can accelerate drug discovery by generating novel molecular structures and predicting their interactions. This integration enhances the efficiency of the drug development pipeline and reduces time-to-market for new therapies.

Medical Imaging Enhancement:

AI-driven medical imaging technologies leverage generative models to improve image resolution, assist in anomaly detection, and generate synthetic medical images for training purposes.

Enhancing Creative Industries

Generative Art and Design:

In the creative industries, generative AI assists artists and designers by generating novel artwork, patterns, and designs. AI tools can collaborate with human creators to explore new artistic styles and techniques.

AI-Driven Content Creation:

For media and entertainment, AI models can generate scripts, music, and visual effects. This integration streamlines content production processes and enables the creation of immersive experiences in film and games.

Advancing Scientific Research

- **Virtual Simulations and Experiments:** Generative AI enables the creation of virtual simulations and experiments, allowing researchers to explore complex phenomena and conduct experiments in virtual environments.
- **Synthetic Data for Research:** AI-generated synthetic data complements real-world datasets, enhancing research in fields with limited data availability. This approach supports more comprehensive analyses and model training.

Future Directions and Innovations

Emerging Technologies and AI Integration

Quantum Computing and AI

The intersection of quantum computing and generative AI holds promise for solving complex optimization problems more efficiently. Quantum algorithms could enhance AI model training and improve performance across various applications.

Edge Computing for Real-Time AI

Edge computing enables real-time data processing and content generation at the network's edge. This integration is particularly valuable for applications requiring low latency, such as autonomous systems and smart devices.

Interdisciplinary Research and Development

Cross-Disciplinary Collaboration:

Fostering interdisciplinary research and collaboration between AI experts, domain specialists, and technology developers can lead to innovative solutions and new applications. Collaborative efforts drive technological advancements and expand the potential of generative AI.

Exploring New Frontiers:

Continued exploration of emerging technologies and interdisciplinary approaches will unlock new possibilities for generative AI. Staying abreast of advancements and fostering a culture of innovation will drive future breakthroughs and applications.

Summary

Integrating generative AI with other advanced technologies offers significant opportunities for enhancing functionality, creating intelligent content, and driving cross-disciplinary innovations. By addressing integration challenges and leveraging the capabilities of technologies such as IoT, cloud computing, and emerging fields, organizations can achieve transformative outcomes and unlock new potentials. As technology continues to evolve, ongoing research and collaboration will play a pivotal role in shaping the future of generative AI and its applications.

Key Takeaways

AI and IoT Integration: Generative AI enhances IoT devices through predictive analytics, real-time data generation, and personalized user experiences. Addressing data privacy, security, and interoperability challenges is essential for successful integration.

AI in Cloud Computing: Cloud computing provides scalable infrastructure, cost efficiency, and collaborative tools for developing and deploying generative AI models. Managed services and big data analytics further support AI applications.

Cross-disciplinary Innovations: Integrating generative AI with healthcare, creative industries, and scientific research leads to personalized solutions, enhanced creativity, and advanced simulations. Interdisciplinary research and emerging technologies drive future innovations.

> **Future Directions:** Exploring quantum computing, edge computing, and fostering cross-disciplinary collaborations will shape the future of generative AI and expand its potential applications.

Part V: The Future of Generative AI

Chapter 15: Emerging Trends in Generative AI

Introduction

Generative AI is rapidly advancing, influencing diverse fields and creating novel applications. This chapter delves into the cutting-edge trends in generative AI, focusing on its role in enhancing creativity, personalizing content, and shaping the metaverse.

AI and Augmented Creativity

Expanding Creative Horizons

AI-Powered Artistic Collaboration:

Generative AI tools are increasingly used to collaborate with artists, offering novel perspectives and techniques that inspire new forms of art. Artists leverage AI to generate unique visual styles, textures, and compositions that might not be conceivable through traditional methods.

Generative Design in Architecture:

AI algorithms assist architects by generating innovative design concepts and structural solutions. These tools analyze vast amounts of architectural data to propose designs that are both aesthetically pleasing and functionally efficient.

Innovative Creative Tools

Advanced Text Generation Models:

AI models like GPT-4 are transforming creative writing by suggesting plot developments, character traits, and dialogue, helping authors to overcome writer's block and explore new storytelling techniques.

Music Generation Platforms:

AI tools for music composition and production offer features such as melody generation, harmony crafting, and rhythm creation, enabling musicians to explore new genres and compositions effortlessly.

Interactive Art and Performance

Dynamic Art Installations:

Generative AI contributes to interactive art installations that adapt to audience interactions and environmental changes. These installations create immersive experiences that evolve in real-time, offering a unique encounter with art.

Live Performance Augmentation:

AI tools are being used to enhance live performances, from generating real-time visuals that sync with music to providing musicians with AI-generated improvisation suggestions during live shows.

Personalized Content Generation

Tailoring Digital Experiences

Enhanced User Profiles:

Generative AI enables the creation of detailed user profiles by analyzing behavior, preferences, and interactions. These profiles help in generating highly personalized content, such as tailored news feeds, product recommendations, and targeted marketing.

Customizable Virtual Environments:

AI tools allow users to design and personalize virtual spaces, such as virtual homes or office environments, according to their tastes and needs, leading to a more engaging and individualized experience.

Adaptive Learning and Personalization

Educational Content Customization:

Generative AI creates personalized educational materials, such as adaptive quizzes and learning modules, based on student performance and learning styles. This approach improves educational outcomes by catering to individual needs.

Personalized Advertising:

AI-driven content generation enables the creation of customized advertisements that resonate with individual preferences and behaviors, enhancing the effectiveness of marketing campaigns.

Enhancing User Engagement

Interactive Virtual Assistants:

AI-powered virtual assistants provide personalized responses and assistance, handling a variety of tasks from scheduling to providing recommendations, based on user preferences and context.

Customized Creative Tools:

AI tools allow users to generate personalized digital content, such as customized greeting cards, artwork, and written pieces, providing creative freedom while ensuring content relevance and uniqueness.

Generative AI in the Metaverse

Crafting Immersive Virtual Worlds

Procedural World Generation:

AI algorithms are used to create expansive and diverse virtual environments in the metaverse. These algorithms generate landscapes, structures, and interactive elements, contributing to a rich and immersive virtual experience.

Dynamic Environment Evolution:

AI models enable virtual worlds to evolve dynamically in response to user interactions and environmental changes, creating a more engaging and adaptive metaverse experience.

Realistic Avatars and NPCs

AI-Generated Avatars:

Generative AI creates realistic and diverse avatars for users in the metaverse, allowing for extensive customization to reflect individual preferences and personalities.

Intelligent Non-Player Characters (NPCs):

AI-driven NPCs exhibit advanced behaviors and responses, enriching interactions and gameplay in the metaverse with lifelike and context-aware characters.

Enhancing Metaverse Experiences

Virtual Reality (VR) Integration:

AI enhances VR experiences by generating realistic virtual objects, environments, and interactions, making virtual worlds more immersive and interactive.

Personalized Virtual Spaces:

AI models customize virtual environments based on user preferences and interactions, providing unique and engaging experiences tailored to individual interests.

Future Directions and Innovations

Advancements in AI Creativity Tools

Next-Generation AI Creativity Platforms:

Future developments in AI creativity platforms will offer more advanced tools for artists, designers, and content creators, including features for real-time collaboration, creative brainstorming, and automated content generation.

Enhanced Personalization Techniques:

Ongoing advancements in personalization techniques will lead to more precise and context-aware content generation, improving user experiences across various digital platforms.

Integration with Emerging Technologies

Augmented Reality (AR) Integration:

Generative AI will play a significant role in enhancing AR experiences by creating dynamic virtual elements that interact seamlessly with the real world.

Metaverse Innovations:

The continued development of the metaverse will see AI driving new innovations in virtual world creation, avatar customization, and interactive experiences, contributing to the evolution of more sophisticated and engaging virtual environments.

Cross-Disciplinary Collaborations

AI and Human Collaboration

Interdisciplinary Projects:

Generative AI is fostering collaborations between different fields, such as combining AI with psychology, neuroscience, and design to explore new creative possibilities and applications.

AI in Scientific Research:

AI tools are being integrated into scientific research to generate hypotheses, analyze complex data sets, and model scientific phenomena, leading to new discoveries and innovations.

AI in Business and Industry

Customized Business Solutions:

Generative AI is being used to create tailored business solutions, such as personalized customer service, automated content creation, and data-driven decision-making tools.

Innovative Product Development:

AI-driven product development processes are enabling companies to design and produce innovative products that meet specific market needs and consumer preferences.

Generative AI

Summary

The emerging trends in generative AI showcase its transformative impact on creativity, personalization, and the metaverse. By enhancing creative processes, tailoring digital experiences, and contributing to the development of immersive virtual worlds, generative AI is reshaping various domains and unlocking new possibilities. As technology advances, continued research and innovation will drive the evolution of generative AI, leading to even more exciting applications and breakthroughs.

Key Takeaways

Augmented Creativity: Generative AI tools are expanding creative boundaries, offering new opportunities for artistic collaboration and innovation across various fields.

Personalized Content: AI-driven personalization techniques are enhancing user engagement by tailoring content to individual preferences and behaviors.

Metaverse Development: Generative AI is contributing to the creation of immersive virtual worlds, realistic avatars, and interactive NPCs, shaping the future of the metaverse.

Future Innovations: Advances in AI creativity tools, personalization techniques, and integration with emerging technologies will drive the evolution of generative AI, leading to new applications and possibilities.

Chapter 16: The Road Ahead

Introduction

Generative AI is evolving rapidly, presenting new opportunities and challenges. This chapter delves into future research directions, potential breakthroughs, and the significant role of generative AI in shaping the future.

Future Research Directions

Advancements in Model Architectures

Next-Generation Architectures:

The pursuit of more sophisticated architectures aims to enhance the capabilities of generative models. Emerging designs, such as more advanced versions of transformers and hybrid models that integrate GANs with VAEs, are expected to improve generative quality and efficiency. Innovations like the incorporation of neural architecture search (NAS) may lead to the discovery of novel, high-performing architectures.

Explainability and Interpretability:

As generative models become more complex, understanding their decision-making processes is crucial. Researchers are developing methods to interpret model outputs, such as attention maps and activation visualization. Explainable AI (XAI) techniques are being integrated to provide insights into how models generate content and make predictions.

Enhancing Data Efficiency

Few-Shot and Zero-Shot Learning:

Future research is focused on enabling generative models to perform effectively with limited training data. Techniques such as meta-learning and transfer learning are being explored to enhance model performance with few-shot or zero-shot scenarios, allowing models to generalize better from minimal examples.

Data Augmentation Techniques:

Advanced data augmentation methods, including synthetic data generation and adversarial training, are being developed to enrich training datasets. These techniques aim to improve model robustness by introducing variability and complexity in the training data.

Ethical and Responsible AI

Bias Mitigation:

Identifying and mitigating biases in generative models is a major research focus. Approaches like fairness constraints, debiasing algorithms, and diverse training datasets are being investigated to ensure that AI systems generate equitable and unbiased outputs.

Regulatory Frameworks:

As generative AI technologies advance, there is a need for comprehensive regulatory frameworks. Researchers and policymakers are working together to establish guidelines that address data privacy, security, and ethical use of AI technologies. This includes developing standards for transparency and accountability in AI systems.

Potential Breakthroughs and Innovations

Advanced Generative Models

Hyper-Realistic Content Generation:

Future breakthroughs may lead to models capable of producing hyper-realistic content across various domains. This includes photorealistic images, high-fidelity audio, and lifelike video. Innovations in neural rendering and high-resolution synthesis are expected to push the boundaries of what generative models can achieve.

Multimodal Generative Models:

Advances in multimodal models that integrate and generate content across different types of data (e.g., text, images, audio) are anticipated. This will enable more seamless and integrated AI applications, allowing for richer and more complex interactions and outputs.

AI for Complex Problem Solving

Generative Design in Engineering:

Generative AI is set to revolutionize engineering through generative design algorithms that optimize structures, materials, and systems. This includes developing new materials with tailored properties and optimizing complex engineering designs for performance and efficiency.

Personalized Medicine:

Breakthroughs in generative AI could transform personalized medicine by enabling the creation of tailored treatment plans and drug formulations based on individual genetic profiles and medical histories. This will lead to more effective and personalized healthcare solutions.

Enhanced Human-AI Collaboration

AI-Augmented Creativity:

Future innovations will likely lead to more sophisticated tools for human-AI collaboration. This includes advanced AI-assisted design tools, creative ideation platforms, and collaborative AI systems that work alongside human creators to enhance artistic and innovative processes.

Interactive AI Systems:

Development of interactive and adaptive AI systems that can engage in meaningful and dynamic interactions with users. These systems will incorporate natural language processing, contextual understanding, and real-time adaptability to provide more intuitive and responsive user experiences.

Generative AI's Role in Shaping the Future

Transforming Industries

Entertainment and Media:

Generative AI is set to continue transforming the entertainment industry by enabling the creation of immersive experiences, high-quality content, and interactive storytelling. This includes advancements in virtual reality (VR) and augmented reality (AR) experiences, as well as AI-generated music, film, and visual arts.

Healthcare:

In healthcare, generative AI will play a crucial role in advancing medical research, personalizing treatments, and improving diagnostic accuracy. This includes developing predictive models for disease progression, creating personalized treatment plans, and enhancing medical imaging and diagnostics.

Redefining Human Experience

Education and Training:

Generative AI will revolutionize education by providing personalized learning experiences and interactive educational tools. AI-driven adaptive learning platforms will tailor educational content to individual learning styles and needs, enhancing the effectiveness of education and training programs.

Workplace Innovation:

The integration of generative AI in the workplace will lead to more efficient workflows, enhanced creativity, and innovative problem-solving approaches. AI tools will support decision-making, automate routine tasks, and foster new forms of collaboration and productivity.

Addressing Global Challenges

Sustainability:

Generative AI can contribute to sustainability efforts by optimizing resource usage, developing eco-friendly materials, and supporting environmental monitoring and management. This includes AI-driven solutions for reducing waste, improving energy efficiency, and managing natural resources.

Social Impact:

AI-driven solutions will address social challenges by improving accessibility for individuals with disabilities, enhancing public safety, and supporting disaster response and recovery efforts. Generative AI technologies will play a role in creating more inclusive and resilient communities.

Summary

The road ahead for generative AI is marked by significant opportunities and challenges. Continued advancements in research, potential breakthroughs, and the expanding role of generative AI across various domains will shape the future of technology and society. As generative AI evolves, it will drive innovation, redefine human experiences, and address global challenges, playing a pivotal role in shaping the future.

Key Takeaways

Advancements in Model Architectures: Future research will focus on developing next-generation architectures and enhancing model interpretability.

Enhanced Data Efficiency: Innovations in few-shot and zero-shot learning, along with advanced data augmentation techniques, will improve generative model performance and robustness.

Ethical and Responsible AI: Addressing biases and developing regulatory frameworks will be essential for the responsible deployment of generative AI technologies.

Potential Breakthroughs: Advanced generative models, multimodal applications, and AI for complex problem-solving will drive significant innovation and impact.

Shaping the Future: Generative AI will continue to transform industries, redefine human experiences, and address global challenges, playing a central role in future advancements and societal changes.

Part VI: Applications and Case Studies

Chapter 17: Hands-On Projects

Introduction

This chapter provides hands-on projects designed to apply generative AI concepts and techniques. By engaging with these practical exercises, you will deepen your understanding of generative models and learn how to implement and adapt these technologies for real-world applications.

Building a Simple GAN from Scratch

Overview

Generative Adversarial Networks (GANs) are composed of two neural networks: a generator and a discriminator. The generator creates synthetic data, while the discriminator evaluates its authenticity. This adversarial setup drives the generator to produce increasingly realistic data as it tries to fool the discriminator.

Project Setup

1. **Install Dependencies:**
   - Ensure you have Python installed, along with TensorFlow or PyTorch for implementing the GAN.
   - Install TensorFlow with the command:

```bash
pip install tensorflow keras
```

2. **Define the Generator and Discriminator:**
   o **Generator:** This neural network generates data from random noise. It learns to produce data samples that resemble the real data distribution.
   o **Discriminator:** This network classifies data as real (from the dataset) or fake (generated by the generator). It learns to distinguish between the two.

Example code snippet for the generator using TensorFlow/Keras:

```python
from tensorflow.keras.models import Sequential
from tensorflow.keras.layers import Dense, LeakyReLU, BatchNormalization, Reshape, Flatten

def build_generator():
    model = Sequential()
    model.add(Dense(256, input_dim=100))
    model.add(LeakyReLU(alpha=0.2))
    model.add(BatchNormalization())
    model.add(Dense(512))
    model.add(LeakyReLU(alpha=0.2))
    model.add(BatchNormalization())
    model.add(Dense(1024))
    model.add(LeakyReLU(alpha=0.2))
```

Generative AI

```
model.add(BatchNormalization())
model.add(Dense(28*28*1, activation='tanh'))
model.add(Reshape((28, 28, 1)))
return model
```

Output:

The build_generator function defines a generator model with multiple dense layers, LeakyReLU activations, batch normalization, and an output layer reshaped to 28x28x1. The output is a TensorFlow/Keras model ready for training.

3. **Compile and Train the GAN:**
   - Train the discriminator with real and fake data to improve its classification accuracy.
   - Train the generator to produce more realistic data by minimizing the discriminator's ability to distinguish between real and fake data.

Example training loop:

```python
def train_gan(generator, discriminator, gan, data, epochs=10000, batch_size=64):
    for epoch in range(epochs):
        # Training the discriminator
        idx = np.random.randint(0, data.shape[0], batch_size)
        real_imgs = data[idx]
        fake_imgs = generator.predict(np.random.randn(batch_size, 100))
        d_loss_real = discriminator.train_on_batch(real_imgs, np.ones((batch_size, 1)))
```

A Comprehensive Guide

```
d_loss_fake = discriminator.train_on_batch(fake_imgs, np.zeros((batch_size, 1)))
d_loss = 0.5 * np.add(d_loss_real, d_loss_fake)

# Training the generator
g_loss = gan.train_on_batch(np.random.randn(batch_size, 100), np.ones((batch_size, 1)))

if epoch % 1000 == 0:
    print(f"Epoch {epoch}: D Loss = {d_loss[0]}, G Loss = {g_loss[0]}")
```

Output:

Every 1000 epochs, the training loop prints the loss values for the discriminator and generator. For instance:

Epoch 0: D Loss = 0.693, G Loss = 0.692

Epoch 1000: D Loss = 0.682, G Loss = 0.693

Epoch 2000: D Loss = 0.678, G Loss = 0.691

Key Considerations

- **Loss Functions:** GANs use loss functions like binary cross-entropy to train both the generator and discriminator. Adjusting these functions can impact model performance.
- **Training Stability:** GANs are notoriously difficult to train due to issues like mode collapse. Techniques such as feature matching and Wasserstein loss can help stabilize training.
- **Evaluation:** Use metrics like Inception Score or Frechet Inception Distance (FID) to assess the quality of generated samples.

Implementing a Text Generator Using GPT

Overview

Generative Pre-trained Transformers (GPT) are advanced models for generating human-like text. They are pre-trained on large datasets and fine-tuned for specific tasks. GPT models can generate coherent and contextually relevant text based on prompts.

Project Setup

1. **Install Dependencies:**
   - Use the Hugging Face Transformers library, which provides pre-trained models and tools for text generation.
   - Install it via pip:

   ```bash
   pip install transformers torch
   ```

2. **Load Pre-trained GPT Model:**
   - Load a pre-trained GPT model and tokenizer from Hugging Face's model hub.
   - Tokenizer converts input text into a format the model can process, while the model generates text based on this input.

Example code snippet for text generation:

```python
from transformers import GPT2LMHeadModel, GPT2Tokenizer

tokenizer = GPT2Tokenizer.from_pretrained('gpt2')
model = GPT2LMHeadModel.from_pretrained('gpt2')
```

A Comprehensive Guide

```
def generate_text(prompt, max_length=100):
    inputs = tokenizer(prompt, return_tensors='pt')
    outputs = model.generate(inputs['input_ids'], max_length=max_length, num_return_sequences=1, temperature=0.7)
    return tokenizer.decode(outputs[0], skip_special_tokens=True)
```

Output:

For the prompt "In a world where technology reigns", you might get an output like:

> In a world where technology reigns, the future is bright and full of possibilities. Advances in artificial intelligence and robotics have transformed everyday life, making tasks easier and more efficient. From self-driving cars to intelligent virtual assistants, technology has revolutionized the way we live and work. However, this rapid progress also brings challenges and ethical considerations that society must address to ensure that technology benefits everyone equally.

3. **Generate Text:**
    - Use the model to generate text based on different prompts.
    - Experiment with various parameters like temperature and top_k to control the creativity and coherence of the output.

Example text generation:

```python
prompt = "In a world where technology reigns"
print(generate_text(prompt))
```

Output:

The code generates an image based on the pre-trained StyleGAN model and saves it as generated_art.png. The output will be a visually appealing image created by the StyleGAN model, which could look like a realistic portrait, abstract art, or any other style the model was trained on.

Key Considerations

- **Model Parameters:** Adjust parameters such as temperature for randomness and top_k for diversity. Higher temperatures produce more creative outputs, while lower temperatures yield more conservative results.
- **Prompt Engineering:** Craft prompts to guide the model towards specific types of responses. Fine-tuning the prompts can significantly affect the generated text quality.
- **Ethical Use:** Ensure that generated text is used responsibly to avoid generating harmful or misleading content.

Creating Art with StyleGAN

Overview

StyleGAN is a powerful generative model designed for creating high-quality images with intricate style and content control. It allows for fine-tuning of various attributes in the generated images, making it suitable for artistic and realistic image creation.

Project Setup

1. **Install Dependencies:**
   - Use the official StyleGAN implementation or libraries such as NVIDIA's repository. Ensure you have CUDA installed for GPU acceleration.
   - Install StyleGAN with pip or clone the repository:

```bash
pip install stylegan2-pytorch
```

2. **Load Pre-trained Model or Train Your Own:**
   - Use a pre-trained StyleGAN model for immediate art generation, or train a new model using your own dataset.
   - Fine-tune the model to adjust attributes like style, color, and features.

Example code for loading and generating images:

```python
from stylegan2_pytorch import StyleGAN2

model = StyleGAN2.load_pretrained('path/to/stylegan2/model')
image = model.generate_image(seed=42)
image.save('generated_art.png')
```

3. **Generate Art:**
   - Experiment with different seeds and parameters to produce diverse and appealing art.
   - Save and visualize the generated images to evaluate the model's performance.

Key Considerations

- **Training Data:** Use diverse datasets to train StyleGAN models to generate a wide range of artistic styles and content.
- **Parameter Tuning:** Adjust parameters like latent vector dimensions and style weights to achieve desired artistic effects.
- **Ethical Use:** Be mindful of the implications of generated art, especially in contexts involving copyright and commercial use.

Summary

Hands-on projects are essential for understanding and mastering generative AI techniques. By building GANs, implementing GPT for text generation, and creating art with StyleGAN, you gain practical experience and insights into the workings of these advanced models. Each project offers opportunities to explore the capabilities and limitations of generative AI, preparing you for more complex applications and innovations.

Key Takeaways

Practical Experience: Engaging in hands-on projects like GANs, text generators, and StyleGAN art creation enhances your understanding and skills in generative AI.

Technical Skills: These projects develop your technical expertise in model implementation, training, and parameter tuning.

Creative Applications: Generative AI offers vast potential for creative exploration and real-world applications, from generating realistic images to crafting compelling text.

Chapter 18: Generative AI in Computer Vision

Introduction

Generative AI has revolutionized the field of computer vision, empowering machines to not only analyze and interpret visual data but also create and enhance visual content in ways that were once thought impossible. This chapter explores the various applications of generative AI in computer vision, detailing how these advanced technologies work and their implications across different industries. By the end of this chapter, readers will gain a comprehensive understanding of image synthesis, deepfake creation and detection, super-resolution imaging, style transfer, artistic creation, and 3D model generation.

Image Synthesis and Enhancement: Creating and Refining Visual Content

Image Synthesis: Generating Realistic and Novel Visuals

Image synthesis involves the generation of new images using AI models, particularly Generative Adversarial Networks (GANs). The process is driven by a generator that creates images and a discriminator that evaluates them, leading to increasingly realistic outcomes through an adversarial learning process. This technique can produce highly realistic images, such as human faces or entire landscapes, which are indistinguishable from real photographs.

Applications:

- **Entertainment:** Creation of realistic visual effects for movies, video games, and virtual reality.
- **Product Design:** Generation of product prototypes and visualizations for industries like automotive and fashion.

Image Enhancement: Improving Image Quality and Clarity

Image enhancement uses AI to refine and improve existing images by increasing resolution, reducing noise, and restoring lost details. Through deep learning, models can identify and correct imperfections, making images clearer and more detailed. This is particularly useful in fields where image quality is crucial, such as medical imaging or satellite imagery.

Applications:

- **Medical Imaging:** Enhancing the clarity of MRI and CT scans for better diagnostic accuracy.
- **Photography:** Automatically improving image quality by adjusting lighting, removing noise, and enhancing resolution.

DeepFakes: Creation and Detection in the Digital Age

Creation of DeepFakes: Manipulating Media with AI

Deepfakes are AI-generated synthetic media where a person's likeness is convincingly replaced with another's in videos, images, or audio. By leveraging GANs and autoencoders, deepfake technology can create highly realistic yet entirely fake content, such as swapping faces in videos or altering speech patterns. While this has legitimate uses in entertainment, it also poses significant risks for misinformation and privacy.

Applications:

- **Entertainment:** De-aging actors in films or creating digital performances.
- **Virtual Influencers:** Generating lifelike digital personas for social media.

Detection of DeepFakes: Safeguarding Truth in Media

The rise of deepfakes has necessitated the development of advanced detection techniques. These methods often involve machine learning models that can identify inconsistencies in deepfake media, such as unnatural facial movements or mismatches in audio and video. The ability to detect deepfakes is crucial for combating misinformation and protecting personal and public integrity.

Applications:

- **Cybersecurity:** Identifying and mitigating the spread of deepfakes in online platforms.
- **Law Enforcement:** Verifying the authenticity of digital evidence in criminal investigations.

Super-Resolution Imaging: Elevating Image Detail and Quality

Techniques in Super-Resolution: From Blurry to Clear

Super-resolution imaging enhances the resolution of images, allowing for more detailed and clearer visuals. Traditional methods often result in blurry images, but generative AI models, especially GANs, can generate high-resolution versions of low-resolution inputs by learning the intricate relationships between image pairs. This technique is critical in fields requiring precise and detailed imagery.

Applications:

- **Remote Sensing:** Enhancing satellite imagery for better environmental monitoring and urban planning.
- **Surveillance:** Improving the resolution of security footage for clearer identification of individuals and objects.

Applications in Industry: Broadening the Impact

Super-resolution has far-reaching applications across various industries. In healthcare, it enables doctors to see finer details in medical images, potentially leading to earlier and more accurate diagnoses. In entertainment, it upscales low-resolution content to meet the demands of modern high-definition displays, improving the overall viewing experience.

Applications:

- **Healthcare:** Enhancing diagnostic images to reveal more detailed information.
- **Consumer Electronics:** Upscaling video content for higher-definition displays.

Style Transfer and Artistic Creation: Merging Art and Technology

Style Transfer: Blending Artistic Styles with Reality

Style transfer is a process where the style of one image (e.g., a painting) is applied to the content of another (e.g., a photograph), creating a unique hybrid image. This technique, powered by deep neural networks, separates the content and style of images and then recombines them to produce visually stunning results. Artists and designers use this to create new works that blend traditional art with modern photography.

Applications:

- **Graphic Design:** Creating visually compelling images that combine the realism of photographs with the styles of famous paintings.
- **Social Media:** Users generate personalized, artistic filters for photos and videos.

Artistic Creation: AI as a Creative Partner

Beyond style transfer, AI is increasingly being used to generate original works of art. Artists are using AI to explore new creative possibilities, generating novel visual and musical compositions that push the boundaries of traditional art forms. These AI-generated pieces are gaining recognition in the art world, with some even being auctioned for significant sums.

Applications:

- **Art Exhibitions:** Displaying AI-generated artworks that challenge traditional notions of creativity.
- **Music Composition:** Using AI to compose original music or assist in the creative process.

3D Model Generation: Building the Future in Three Dimensions

Generative Models for 3D: From Pixels to Polygons

Generative AI models are now capable of creating 3D models from 2D images or textual descriptions, revolutionizing fields like gaming, architecture, and robotics. These models, particularly 3D GANs and variational autoencoders, can generate detailed 3D representations of objects and scenes, significantly reducing the time and effort required for manual 3D modeling.

Applications:

- **Gaming:** Rapid generation of complex 3D environments and characters for video games.
- **Architecture:** Automating the design of intricate structures and urban layouts.

Applications in Industry: Transforming Design and Manufacturing

In industries like automotive design and robotics, generative AI is used to create and test 3D models before they are physically built. This not only speeds up the design process but also allows for more innovative and optimized designs. For example, in robotics, AI can generate and simulate different components, ensuring they work as intended before manufacturing.

Applications:

- **Automotive Design:** Creating and testing vehicle prototypes in a virtual environment.
- **Robotics:** Simulating robotic components and environments for testing and optimization.

Summary

Generative AI is fundamentally transforming computer vision by enabling machines to create, enhance, and interpret visual content in ways that were previously unimaginable. From synthesizing new images and enhancing their quality to creating and detecting deepfakes, transferring artistic styles, and generating 3D models, the applications are vast and impactful. While these advancements open up exciting possibilities, they also bring challenges, particularly in terms of ethics and security. As this technology continues to evolve, it will play an increasingly vital role in shaping the future of visual computing.

Key Takeaways

Image Synthesis and Enhancement:

Generative AI enables the creation of realistic images from scratch.

AI-driven enhancement techniques improve image quality and clarity, with applications in entertainment, medical diagnostics, and more.

DeepFakes: Creation and Detection:

Deepfake technology showcases the creative potential of generative AI but also highlights ethical challenges.

Robust detection methods are essential to combat misinformation and maintain trust in digital media.

Super-Resolution Imaging:

Generative AI enhances image resolution, making it indispensable in fields requiring precise visual detail, such as remote sensing and medical imaging.

Style Transfer and Artistic Creation:

AI-driven style transfer merges artistic styles with real-world content, creating unique visual experiences.

Generative AI expands the boundaries of creativity, serving as a collaborator in producing original artworks and compositions.

3D Model Generation:

Generative AI

Generative AI revolutionizes 3D modeling by enabling the rapid creation of detailed models from 2D images or descriptions.

This technology accelerates design processes across industries, from gaming to automotive design and robotics.

Chapter 19: Generative AI in Natural Language Processing

Introduction

Generative AI has transformed Natural Language Processing (NLP) by enhancing how machines generate, understand, and interact with human language. This chapter explores key applications of generative AI in NLP, including text generation and summarization, conversational agents and chatbots, machine translation, content creation and copywriting, and sentiment and emotion analysis.

Text Generation and Summarization

Text Generation

Text generation refers to the creation of new, contextually relevant text based on given inputs. Generative AI models, especially those based on deep learning, have revolutionized this field. Key technologies include:

- **Transformers:** Models like GPT-4 (Generative Pre-trained Transformer 4) have set new standards in text generation by leveraging large-scale datasets to produce coherent and contextually appropriate text. These models are pre-trained on diverse data sources and fine-tuned for specific tasks or domains.

- **Applications:**
  - **Creative Writing:** AI-generated content can include anything from fiction and poetry to scripts and screenplays. For instance, AI tools can assist authors by suggesting plot ideas, dialogue, and narrative elements.
  - **Automated Content Creation:** News articles, reports, and blog posts can be generated quickly, saving time and reducing the workload for content creators. Automated tools can draft content based on a brief, ensuring consistency and efficiency.
  - **Personalized Content:** Generative AI can tailor content to individual user preferences, enhancing engagement by creating personalized recommendations, email content, and product descriptions.

Text Summarization

Summarization involves distilling a larger piece of text into a shorter, concise version, maintaining the core message and context. Techniques used include:

- **Extractive Summarization:** This method involves identifying and extracting key sentences or phrases from the original text. Algorithms assess sentence importance based on factors like frequency and placement. For example, news aggregation services use extractive summarization to provide concise news summaries.
- **Abstractive Summarization:** Unlike extractive summarization, abstractive techniques generate new sentences to convey the essence of the original text. This approach often results in more natural-sounding summaries and can involve sophisticated models like BERT (Bidirectional Encoder Representations from Transformers) and T5 (Text-To-Text Transfer Transformer).

Conversational Agents and Chatbots

Conversational Agents

Conversational agents, powered by generative AI, simulate human conversation, allowing users to interact with machines as if they were engaging with another person. Key features include:

- **Natural Language Understanding (NLU):** This involves interpreting user inputs, including intent and context, to generate appropriate responses. Modern NLU systems use deep learning models to understand nuances in language, such as idiomatic expressions and contextual references.
- **Dialogue Management:** Effective dialogue management systems handle conversation flow, ensuring that interactions remain coherent and contextually relevant. These systems maintain context across multiple turns of conversation, allowing for more natural interactions.
- **Applications:**
  - **Customer Support:** AI-driven chatbots handle routine customer queries, provide troubleshooting guidance, and escalate complex issues to human agents. This increases the efficiency and availability of support services.
  - **Personal Assistants:** Virtual assistants like Siri, Alexa, and Google Assistant help with tasks such as setting reminders, answering questions, and managing schedules. These assistants use conversational AI to provide relevant and timely assistance.
  - **Therapeutic Conversations:** AI-based therapy bots offer mental health support by engaging users in therapeutic conversations, providing coping strategies, and offering emotional support.

Chatbots

Chatbots are a subset of conversational agents specifically designed for handling predefined interactions. They can be:

- **Rule-Based:** These chatbots follow predefined scripts and rules, responding to specific keywords or phrases. They are suitable for handling simple queries and tasks but lack flexibility in understanding context.
- **AI-Powered:** AI-driven chatbots use machine learning to understand and respond to a wider range of inputs. They can learn from interactions and improve over time, offering more sophisticated responses and handling complex queries.

Machine Translation

Machine translation involves automatically translating text from one language to another. Recent advancements in generative AI have transformed this field:

Neural Machine Translation (NMT)

NMT models use neural networks to provide high-quality translations by considering the context of entire sentences rather than just individual words. Key features include:

- **Contextual Understanding:** NMT models, such as those based on the Transformer architecture, handle long-range dependencies and context more effectively than previous models, leading to more accurate translations.
- **Real-Time Translation:** Advanced NMT systems enable real-time translation of spoken or written text, facilitating cross-lingual communication in applications like instant messaging and video conferencing.
- **Applications:**
    - **Online Translation Services:** Tools like Google Translate and DeepL provide instant translation of text, webpages, and documents, making information accessible across different languages.
    - **Multilingual Customer Support:** NMT helps businesses offer support in multiple languages, improving customer experience and accessibility.

- o **Cross-Lingual Content Creation:** Content can be adapted for different linguistic and cultural contexts, expanding reach and engagement.

Content Creation and Copywriting

Generative AI has become an invaluable tool in content creation and copywriting, offering automated solutions for producing engaging and persuasive text:

Content Creation

Generative AI aids in various aspects of content creation, including:

- **Idea Generation:** AI tools can suggest topics, headlines, and angles for content based on trends, audience preferences, and historical data. This streamlines the brainstorming process and ensures relevance.
- **Drafting:** AI models can generate drafts for articles, blog posts, and reports based on input parameters. These drafts can be refined and customized to meet specific requirements.
- **Optimization:** AI-driven tools can optimize content for readability, SEO, and engagement by suggesting improvements and providing insights into audience preferences.

Copywriting

In copywriting, generative AI enhances the creation of compelling marketing and advertising text:

- **Headlines and Taglines:** AI can generate catchy and memorable headlines and taglines that capture attention and drive interest.
- **Persuasive Copy:** AI models help craft persuasive marketing copy that resonates with target audiences, driving conversions and engagement.

- **Personalization:** AI can tailor marketing messages to different audience segments, enhancing relevance and effectiveness.

Sentiment and Emotion Analysis

Sentiment and emotion analysis involves interpreting the emotional tone and sentiment expressed in text. Generative AI provides sophisticated tools for this analysis:

Sentiment Analysis

Sentiment analysis involves classifying text into categories such as positive, negative, or neutral. Key features include:

- **Accuracy:** Advanced AI models improve accuracy in sentiment classification by understanding context and nuances in language.
- **Applications:**
  - **Customer Feedback:** Analyzing reviews and feedback to gauge customer satisfaction and identify areas for improvement.
  - **Social Media Monitoring:** Assessing public sentiment about brands, products, or events to inform business strategies.

Emotion Analysis

Emotion analysis goes beyond sentiment to identify specific emotions expressed in text, such as joy, sadness, or anger. Key features include:

- **Detailed Insights:** Provides a deeper understanding of emotional responses, helping businesses and researchers gain insights into consumer sentiments and reactions.
- **Applications:**
  - **Market Research:** Understanding consumer emotions to inform product development and marketing strategies.

- **Crisis Management:** Detecting and addressing negative sentiments or emotional distress in real-time to manage brand reputation and customer relations.

Summary

Generative AI has profoundly impacted various aspects of Natural Language Processing, from text generation and summarization to conversational agents, machine translation, content creation, and sentiment analysis. These advancements have not only improved the quality and efficiency of language-related tasks but also opened new opportunities for innovation and personalization.

The integration of generative AI in NLP continues to evolve, offering increasingly sophisticated solutions for understanding and generating human language. As these technologies advance, they will likely play an even more critical role in shaping how we communicate, create, and interact with text and language.

Key Takeaways

Generative AI significantly enhances text generation, summarization, and personalization, improving content creation and engagement.

Conversational agents and chatbots leverage AI to provide natural and contextually relevant interactions, transforming customer support and personal assistance.

Machine translation has become more accurate and contextually aware, facilitating cross-lingual communication and accessibility.

AI-driven content creation and copywriting tools streamline the production of engaging and persuasive text, optimizing marketing and communication efforts.

Sentiment and emotion analysis powered by generative AI provides deeper insights into user feedback and emotional responses, supporting better decision-making and customer relations.

Chapter 20: Generative AI in Art and Creativity

Introduction

Generative AI is transforming the landscape of art and creativity, offering innovative tools and techniques that expand traditional creative boundaries. This chapter explores the impact of AI on various creative fields, including music, visual arts, film, animation, design, and writing, and highlights case studies that demonstrate the potential of AI-driven collaborations with artists.

AI-Generated Music and Art

AI-Generated Music

Generative AI has revolutionized music composition by leveraging models like OpenAI's MuseNet and Google's Magenta. These models use deep learning algorithms to analyze vast amounts of music data, learning patterns, structures, and styles to create original compositions. AI tools can generate entire pieces of music in various genres, provide accompaniment to existing melodies, or even assist in composing personalized tracks based on user preferences. Additionally, AI-driven music generation tools enable real-time music creation and interactive experiences, such as AI-powered music improvisation or live performance enhancements.

Key Technologies

- **Recurrent Neural Networks (RNNs):** Used for sequential data processing, ideal for generating melodies and rhythms.
- **Generative Adversarial Networks (GANs):** Employed to create novel music by pitting two neural networks against each other, one generating music and the other evaluating its quality.
- **Variational Autoencoders (VAEs):** Used for exploring latent spaces in music, allowing for the generation of diverse musical styles.

AI-Generated Art

In visual arts, generative AI uses techniques like Generative Adversarial Networks (GANs) and neural style transfer to create and manipulate artwork. GANs can generate new images based on training data, producing artworks that range from abstract pieces to photorealistic portraits. Neural style transfer applies the artistic style of one image to the content of another, enabling artists to create unique hybrid artworks. AI art tools also assist in art restoration and enhancement, reconstructing damaged or incomplete artworks with remarkable accuracy.

Key Technologies

- **Generative Adversarial Networks (GANs):** Generate high-quality images by learning from a dataset of existing art.
- **Neural Style Transfer:** Combines the content of one image with the artistic style of another, creating visually appealing results.
- **DeepDream:** Uses convolutional neural networks to enhance and modify images, often producing surreal and intricate patterns.

AI in Film and Animation

Film

Generative AI enhances film production across several domains, including scriptwriting, visual effects (VFX), and character creation. AI-driven tools assist in automating scriptwriting by generating dialogue and plot elements based on genre-specific models. In VFX, AI helps with tasks like deepfake creation and scene synthesis, enabling realistic visual effects and simplifying complex post-production processes. AI can also create virtual actors and digital doubles, offering filmmakers new ways to visualize and execute creative concepts.

Key Technologies

- **Natural Language Processing (NLP):** Used for scriptwriting and dialogue generation by analyzing existing scripts and generating coherent narrative elements.
- **Deep Learning Models:** Employed for VFX, including deepfake technology and scene reconstruction.
- **Generative Models:** Create digital doubles and virtual actors by learning from extensive datasets of human movement and expression.

Animation

In animation, AI facilitates tasks such as character animation, storyboarding, and style adaptation. AI tools automate the generation of animation frames, improving efficiency and consistency in character movements. Additionally, AI assists in creating dynamic storyboards and visualizing scenes by predicting and filling in gaps based on existing content. Style adaptation tools allow animators to apply various artistic styles to their animations, enabling diverse visual experiences.

Key Technologies

- **Pose Estimation:** Used to track and animate character movements based on predefined positions and actions.

- **Frame Interpolation:** Enhances animation by generating intermediate frames between existing ones, resulting in smoother motion.
- **Style Transfer:** Applies different artistic styles to animation frames, offering varied visual effects.

Generative Design in Architecture and Fashion

Architecture

Generative AI in architecture enables architects to explore diverse design options and optimize structural elements. AI tools use algorithms to analyze and generate architectural designs based on parameters such as spatial requirements, material constraints, and aesthetic preferences. These tools assist in parametric design, where designs are generated based on adjustable parameters, allowing for rapid iteration and exploration of innovative solutions. AI also aids in smart city planning by optimizing infrastructure and urban layouts using predictive analytics.

Key Technologies

- **Parametric Design Tools:** Generate architectural designs based on adjustable parameters and constraints.
- **Optimization Algorithms:** Improve structural efficiency and material usage by analyzing various design scenarios.
- **Predictive Analytics:** Enhance urban planning by forecasting future needs and optimizing infrastructure.

Fashion

In fashion, generative AI is used for designing clothing, predicting trends, and providing personalized recommendations. AI tools can create new fashion designs by learning from existing trends and patterns, allowing designers to explore novel aesthetics and styles. AI-driven trend prediction models analyze social media, market data, and historical trends to forecast upcoming fashion trends. Additionally, virtual try-ons and personalized fashion recommendations enhance the customer experience by providing tailored suggestions and virtual fittings.

Key Technologies

- **Generative Models:** Create new fashion designs by learning from existing collections and trends.
- **Trend Analysis Algorithms:** Forecast future fashion trends based on market data and social media analysis.
- **Virtual Try-Ons:** Use AI to simulate how clothing items will look on individuals, enhancing online shopping experiences.

The Role of AI in Creative Writing

Creative Writing

Generative AI supports creative writing by assisting with plot development, dialogue generation, and editing. AI tools can generate narrative elements, suggest plot twists, and provide feedback on writing style and coherence. These tools use NLP and machine learning to analyze existing literature and generate original content based on user inputs. AI-driven writing assistants also help with grammar, style, and structure, offering real-time suggestions and improvements.

Key Technologies

- **Natural Language Processing (NLP):** Analyzes and generates text, assisting with plot development and dialogue creation.
- **Machine Learning Models:** Provide feedback and suggestions based on an analysis of existing literature and user inputs.
- **Grammar and Style Checkers:** Offer real-time improvements and corrections to enhance writing quality.

Case Studies: AI Collaborations with Artists

Case Study 1: Refik Anadol

Refik Anadol's work demonstrates how AI can be used to create immersive data-driven art. Anadol uses AI algorithms to transform data into dynamic visual experiences, resulting in art installations that interact with viewers and respond to real-time data inputs. His projects, such as "Machine Hallucinations," showcase AI's potential to create innovative and engaging art that challenges traditional boundaries.

Case Study 2: Obvious Art Collective

The Obvious Art Collective's AI-generated artwork "Edmond de Belamy" illustrates how AI can produce marketable and innovative art. The portrait, created using GANs, sold at auction for a substantial sum, highlighting the acceptance of AI-generated art in the art market. This case study demonstrates how AI can challenge traditional notions of creativity and artistic value.

Case Study 3: AI in Music Collaboration

Taryn Southern's collaboration with the AI tool Amper Music in her album "I AM AI" shows how AI can enhance musical creativity. Southern used AI to compose and produce tracks, exploring new musical possibilities and pushing the boundaries of traditional music production. This collaboration highlights AI's potential to offer unique creative opportunities in the music industry.

Summary

Generative AI is reshaping the world of art and creativity, providing innovative tools and techniques that redefine traditional creative processes. From music and visual art to film, animation, architecture, fashion, and writing, AI enhances and expands artistic possibilities, enabling new forms of expression and collaboration. As AI technology continues to evolve, its role in art and creativity will undoubtedly grow, leading to further advancements and new opportunities for artistic exploration.

Key Takeaways

> Generative AI is transforming art and creativity by offering tools that enhance music composition, visual art, film production, animation, design, and writing.
>
> AI enables novel artistic expressions and more efficient production processes, pushing the boundaries of traditional creative practices.
>
> Collaborations between AI and artists illustrate the potential for AI to innovate and inspire, contributing to the evolution of artistic fields and creative industries.

Chapter 21: Case Studies

Introduction

Generative AI represents a transformative force across various domains, offering innovative solutions and reshaping traditional approaches. As these technologies evolve, their real-world applications become increasingly diverse, demonstrating their potential to revolutionize multiple sectors. This chapter explores notable case studies showcasing how generative AI is applied in practice. By examining specific examples, industry-specific implementations, and lessons learned, we gain insights into the practical impact of generative AI and its potential for future development.

Real-World Applications of Generative AI

Generative AI's ability to create new and diverse content has led to its adoption in numerous fields. This section delves into specific applications that highlight its transformative potential:

Art and Entertainment

DALL-E and Artistic Creation

DALL-E, developed by OpenAI, is a powerful example of how generative models can be used to create art. This model generates images from textual descriptions, enabling users to visualize concepts that may not exist in reality. The creative possibilities are vast, from generating fantastical creatures to designing new fashion items. DALL-E's capability to blend imagination with machine learning has opened up new avenues for artistic expression and design.

Use Case

- **Design and Advertising**: Advertising agencies leverage DALL-E to quickly generate diverse visual content for marketing campaigns. This technology allows for rapid prototyping of creative concepts, enabling marketers to explore a wide range of visual ideas and tailor their campaigns to specific audiences.

Case Study

- **Ad Agency Example**: An ad agency used DALL-E to generate several visual concepts for a new product launch. By inputting various creative prompts, the agency was able to present multiple design options to the client in a fraction of the time it would normally take, resulting in a more dynamic and visually engaging campaign.

Healthcare

Drug Discovery

Generative models, particularly GANs, have made significant strides in drug discovery by generating novel molecular structures. These models learn from extensive datasets of chemical compounds to propose new molecules with potential therapeutic effects. This accelerates the drug discovery process, reducing time and costs associated with traditional methods.

Use Case

Pharmaceutical Companies: Companies like Insilico Medicine utilize generative models to identify promising drug candidates for complex diseases. By generating and screening thousands of potential compounds, these models help researchers focus on the most promising candidates, speeding up the path from discovery to clinical trials.

Case Study

Insilico Medicine: Insilico Medicine applied GANs to discover new molecules for cancer treatment. The use of generative models allowed the company to identify novel compounds more efficiently, resulting in the advancement of several candidates to preclinical testing stages.

Text Generation and NLP

GPT-3 and Content Creation

GPT-3, developed by OpenAI, is a state-of-the-art text generation model capable of producing coherent and contextually relevant text. Its applications span various domains, including content creation, customer service, and educational tools. The model's ability to generate human-like text has revolutionized writing and communication tasks.

Use Case

Content Creation Platforms: Platforms like Jasper and Copy.ai leverage GPT-3 to assist users in generating marketing copy, blog posts, and other types of content. This technology enhances productivity by automating content generation, allowing creators to focus on higher-level tasks.

Case Study

Copy.ai: Copy.ai used GPT-3 to develop a tool that helps businesses create engaging marketing content. By integrating the model into their platform, they provided users with a powerful writing assistant capable of generating high-quality text based on minimal input.

Image and Video Synthesis

Deepfake Technology

Deepfake technology, powered by GANs, allows for the creation of highly realistic synthetic media, including images and videos. While it has applications in entertainment and social media, it also raises ethical concerns related to misinformation and privacy.

Use Case

Entertainment Industry: The film industry uses deepfake technology for special effects, such as de-aging actors or recreating deceased performers. This allows for more creative storytelling and visual effects without the limitations of traditional techniques.

Case Study

The Irishman: The film "The Irishman" employed deepfake technology to de-age actors, allowing them to portray their characters over several decades. The result was a visually seamless film that utilized advanced technology to enhance storytelling.

Industry-Specific Implementations

Generative AI's impact extends across various industries, each leveraging its capabilities to achieve specific goals. This section explores how different sectors are implementing generative AI:

Finance

Algorithmic Trading

In finance, generative models are used to simulate market conditions and develop trading strategies. By generating synthetic financial data, these models help traders test and optimize algorithms under diverse scenarios, improving their robustness and performance.

Use Case

Investment Firms: Firms use generative models to forecast market trends and optimize trading strategies. For example, models like GANs can simulate different market conditions, allowing traders to evaluate their strategies and adapt to potential future scenarios.

Case Study

Goldman Sachs: Goldman Sachs incorporated generative models into their trading systems to simulate market conditions and test trading algorithms. This approach enhanced their ability to anticipate market changes and refine their trading strategies.

Education

Personalized Learning

Generative AI is used in education to create customized learning experiences. By analyzing students' progress and preferences, generative models generate personalized educational content, such as quizzes, exercises, and learning paths.

Use Case

EdTech Companies: Companies like Duolingo use generative AI to provide tailored learning experiences. The technology adapts to each student's learning style and progress, offering personalized lessons that enhance engagement and effectiveness.

Case Study

Khan Academy: Khan Academy implemented generative AI to create personalized learning paths for students. By analyzing performance data, the system generates customized exercises and recommendations, helping students achieve better learning outcomes.

Retail

Product Design and Customization

In retail, generative AI assists in designing new products and personalizing customer experiences. By analyzing customer data and preferences, these models generate product designs and recommend tailored options.

Use Case

E-commerce Platforms: Platforms like Nike use generative AI to offer personalized product recommendations and custom designs. The technology helps customers visualize and create products that meet their individual tastes and preferences.

Case Study

Nike By You: Nike's "Nike By You" platform uses generative AI to allow customers to design their own shoes. By providing a range of customization options, the platform offers a personalized shopping experience and enhances customer satisfaction.

Lessons Learned from Successful Projects

Examining successful generative AI projects provides valuable insights into best practices and strategies. Here are key lessons learned:

Data Quality and Diversity

Importance of High-Quality Data

Generative models require high-quality and diverse datasets to produce effective results. Successful projects emphasize the importance of data quality, ensuring that models are trained on comprehensive and representative datasets.

Lesson Learned

Invest in Data Collection: High-quality data collection and curation are critical for training effective generative models. Ensuring that datasets are diverse and representative of the target domain improves model performance and output quality.

Ethical Considerations

Addressing Ethical Challenges

Ethical considerations, including bias and privacy, are crucial when deploying generative AI. Successful projects incorporate mechanisms to address these challenges, ensuring responsible and fair use of technology.

Lesson Learned

Implement Ethical Guidelines: Developing and adhering to ethical guidelines helps address potential issues related to bias, misinformation, and privacy. Incorporating ethical considerations into the development process ensures responsible AI deployment.

Continuous Improvement

Iterative Development

Generative AI projects benefit from iterative development and continuous refinement. Regular updates and feedback incorporation help enhance model performance and applicability.

Lesson Learned

Adopt an Agile Approach: Using an iterative approach allows for continuous improvement of generative models. Regularly updating models based on user feedback and performance metrics leads to better results and increased effectiveness.

Summary

Generative AI has made a profound impact across various sectors, demonstrating its potential to revolutionize traditional approaches and create innovative solutions. By exploring real-world applications, industry-specific implementations, and lessons learned from successful projects, we gain valuable insights into the practical applications and challenges of generative AI. Its transformative capabilities highlight the need for ongoing development, ethical considerations, and continuous improvement, ensuring that generative AI continues to drive progress and innovation in the future.

Key Takeaways

> **Transformative Potential**: Generative AI's applications span diverse fields, including art, healthcare, finance, education, and retail, showcasing its versatility and impact.
>
> **Industry-Specific Benefits**: Different industries leverage generative AI to enhance operations, create personalized experiences, and drive innovation.
>
> **Data and Ethics**: High-quality data and ethical considerations are crucial for the successful and responsible deployment of generative AI.
>
> **Iterative Improvement**: Continuous development and refinement of generative models lead to better performance and applicability.

Part VII: Framework, Platform, and Tools

Chapter 22: Tools and Platforms for Generative AI

Introduction

Generative AI is transforming industries by enabling machines to create content, from text and images to music and more. However, the success of generative AI projects largely depends on the tools and platforms used. This chapter explores the leading frameworks, platforms, and specialized libraries that power generative AI, providing a comprehensive guide to help you choose the right resources for your projects.

Overview of Popular Generative AI Frameworks

Generative AI frameworks provide the essential building blocks for developing and experimenting with AI models. Below, we delve into the most widely used frameworks, outlining their key features, strengths, and generative AI capabilities.

TensorFlow

Overview
TensorFlow, developed by Google Brain, is one of the most powerful open-source libraries for machine learning and deep learning. It is

known for its flexibility and scalability, making it a go-to choice for both research and production.

Generative AI Capabilities

TensorFlow offers tools like TensorFlow GAN (TF-GAN) for building and training Generative Adversarial Networks (GANs) and TensorFlow Probability for probabilistic models, including Variational Autoencoders (VAEs).

Strengths

- **Scalability**: Suitable for large-scale distributed computing.
- **Integration**: Seamless integration with other Google services and tools like TensorBoard for visualization.
- **Community Support**: Extensive documentation, tutorials, and a large community of developers.

PyTorch

Overview

PyTorch, developed by Facebook's AI Research lab, has gained popularity for its dynamic computational graph, which makes it easier to debug and experiment with models. It's particularly favored in the research community.

Generative AI Capabilities

PyTorch supports the development of GANs, VAEs, and other generative models. Pyro, a probabilistic programming library built on PyTorch, is used for deep probabilistic modeling.

Strengths

- **Dynamic Computation Graphs**: Allows for flexible model building and debugging.
- **Research-Oriented**: Preferred by academics for its ease of experimentation.

- **Interoperability**: Compatible with NumPy, making it easier to transition between frameworks.

Keras

Overview

Keras is a high-level API for building and training deep learning models, originally developed by François Chollet. It is designed for ease of use, with an intuitive interface that enables rapid experimentation.

Generative AI Capabilities

Keras can be used to build GANs and VAEs, with various examples and tutorials available for beginners.

Strengths:

1. **Simplicity**: User-friendly API that simplifies complex tasks.
2. **Flexibility**: Can run on top of TensorFlow, Theano, or CNTK.
3. **Rapid Prototyping**: Ideal for quickly building and testing models.

Hugging Face Transformers

Overview

Hugging Face's Transformers library has revolutionized natural language processing (NLP) by providing easy access to pre-trained models, including those for generative tasks like text generation.

Generative AI Capabilities

The library includes models like GPT-3, BERT, and T5, which are state-of-the-art in text generation and other NLP tasks.

Strengths:

- **Pre-Trained Models**: A vast repository of pre-trained models that can be fine-tuned for specific tasks.
- **Ease of Use**: Simple API for loading, training, and deploying models.
- **Community Support**: Extensive documentation and a strong community contributing to the development of new models.

Platforms for Training and Deploying Models

Deploying and scaling generative AI models require robust platforms that can handle intensive computational tasks. This section reviews some of the leading cloud platforms for training and deploying AI models, focusing on their features and advantages.

Google Cloud AI Platform

Overview: Google Cloud AI Platform provides a comprehensive suite of tools for developing, training, and deploying machine learning models. It supports a wide range of frameworks, including TensorFlow, PyTorch, and Keras.

Generative AI Capabilities: The platform offers managed services for training and deploying models, including support for custom containers and Kubernetes-based serving.

Strengths:

- **Integration with Google Tools**: Seamless integration with other Google Cloud services, such as BigQuery and Dataflow.
- **Advanced Tools**: Features like AutoML and AI Hub allow for automated model training and sharing.
- **Security**: Strong security features, including identity management and data encryption.

AWS SageMaker

Overview: AWS SageMaker is a fully managed service that covers the entire machine learning lifecycle, from building and training models to deployment. It supports popular frameworks like TensorFlow, PyTorch, and MXNet.

Generative AI Capabilities: SageMaker offers pre-built algorithms for generative tasks, managed training environments, and endpoints for real-time inference.

Strengths:

- **Comprehensive Tools**: Includes everything needed for machine learning, from data labeling to model tuning and deployment.
- **Scalability**: Easily scale your models from single-instance training to distributed training across multiple nodes.
- **Ecosystem Integration**: Integrates well with other AWS services, such as S3 for storage and Lambda for serverless computing.

Microsoft Azure Machine Learning

Overview: Azure Machine Learning is a cloud-based service that enables developers and data scientists to build, train, and deploy machine learning models. It supports various frameworks, including TensorFlow, PyTorch, and Scikit-learn.

Generative AI Capabilities: Azure ML provides automated machine learning (AutoML) for quick model development, as well as tools for model deployment and monitoring.

Strengths:

- **Integrated Tools**: Includes tools for data preparation, feature engineering, and model monitoring.
- **Ease of Use**: User-friendly interface and pre-configured environments for rapid development.

- **Scalability and Performance**: High-performance computing capabilities, including support for GPUs and TPUs.

Comparative Analysis of Tools and Libraries

Choosing the right tool or library is crucial for the success of your generative AI project. This section provides a comparative analysis of the most popular tools, highlighting their suitability for different tasks and use cases.

Overview of Popular Tools (e.g., TensorFlow, PyTorch, JAX)

TensorFlow:

Strengths: TensorFlow is a comprehensive, end-to-end open-source platform for machine learning. It is particularly well-suited for large-scale production models due to its mature ecosystem, which includes TensorFlow Serving for model deployment, TensorFlow Lite for mobile and embedded devices, and TensorFlow Extended (TFX) for production ML pipelines.

Use Cases: TensorFlow is ideal for projects requiring robust deployment options, scalability, and extensive community support. It excels in production environments where stability and support are crucial.

Limitations: TensorFlow's initial learning curve can be steep, and while it has improved over the years, some developers find it less intuitive than PyTorch.

PyTorch:

Strengths: PyTorch is known for its flexibility and ease of use, particularly in research and experimentation. Its dynamic computation graph (also known as define-by-run) allows for more intuitive model building and debugging. PyTorch also integrates well with the Python ecosystem, making it a favorite among researchers and academic institutions.

Use Cases: PyTorch is ideal for projects that involve a lot of experimentation, custom model architectures, or require rapid iteration. It's widely used in cutting-edge research and is often the first choice for developing novel AI techniques.

Limitations: While PyTorch has made strides in production readiness with tools like TorchServe and ONNX, it is still perceived as more research-oriented compared to TensorFlow.

JAX:

Strengths: JAX is a newer library that brings together NumPy's API with automatic differentiation, making it a powerful tool for researchers focused on high-performance computing. JAX is particularly effective for tasks that require fast execution and parallelization, such as gradient-based optimization in large-scale models.

Use Cases: JAX is suitable for projects that demand performance optimization and seamless integration with NumPy. It is gaining traction in research areas where performance and flexibility are critical.

Limitations: JAX's ecosystem is still growing, and while it's powerful, it doesn't yet have the extensive toolset and community support that TensorFlow and PyTorch offer.

Specialized Libraries for GANs, VAEs, and Transformers

GANs:

TensorFlow GAN: Provides a comprehensive toolkit for building GANs, including pre-built architectures, training utilities, and support for custom models. TensorFlow GAN leverages TensorFlow's ecosystem for training and deployment, making it a strong choice for production-level GAN projects.

PyTorch-GAN: Offers a range of GAN implementations with a focus on research and experimentation. PyTorch-GAN is ideal for developers who want to quickly prototype and test new GAN architectures with the flexibility of PyTorch.

VAEs:

TensorFlow Probability: Combines TensorFlow with probabilistic modeling tools, making it ideal for developing Variational Autoencoders (VAEs). It supports advanced techniques like Bayesian neural networks and stochastic variational inference.

Pyro: A probabilistic programming library built on PyTorch, Pyro is designed for deep probabilistic models like VAEs. It is particularly suited for research applications that require custom probabilistic models and complex inference techniques.

Transformers:

Hugging Face Transformers: The go-to library for building and fine-tuning Transformer-based models, particularly in natural language processing (NLP). Hugging Face Transformers provides pre-trained models, a user-friendly API, and extensive documentation, making it the preferred choice for NLP tasks.

T5 and BERT in TensorFlow: TensorFlow also supports Transformer models like T5 and BERT, providing tools for training and fine-tuning these models within TensorFlow's ecosystem. This is particularly useful for projects that require integration with other TensorFlow tools.

Using Pre-trained Models and Transfer Learning

Pre-trained Models

Advantages: Pre-trained models like GPT-3, BERT, and StyleGAN offer a head start by providing models that have already been trained on large datasets. These models can be fine-tuned for specific tasks, significantly reducing development time and computational resources.

Use Cases: Pre-trained models are ideal for tasks where obtaining and training on large datasets would be impractical, such as in NLP, image synthesis, and style transfer. They allow developers to leverage state-of-the-art performance without needing extensive computational infrastructure.

Transfer Learning

Concept: Transfer learning involves taking a pre-trained model and adapting it to a new but related task. This approach is particularly effective when you have limited data for your specific task but can leverage knowledge from a related domain.

Benefits: Transfer learning reduces training time and improves performance, especially in tasks where labeled data is scarce. It is widely used in applications like image classification, object detection, and NLP.

Building and Training Your Generative AI Models

Model Construction

Framework Selection: The choice of framework (TensorFlow, PyTorch, or JAX) should align with your project's requirements, considering factors like scalability, flexibility, and the need for custom architectures. For example, TensorFlow might be preferred for enterprise applications, while PyTorch could be better for research-oriented projects.

Architecture Definition: Use the chosen framework's tools to define your model's architecture. For generative models, this might involve designing the generator and discriminator for GANs or the encoder and decoder for VAEs.

Training Considerations

Data Quality: High-quality, well-preprocessed data is critical for successful model training. This includes tasks like normalization, augmentation, and balancing datasets to avoid overfitting.

Computational Resources: Utilize GPUs or TPUs to accelerate training, especially for deep networks. Tools like TensorFlow's Model Parallelism or PyTorch's DataParallel can help distribute training across multiple devices.

Optimization Techniques: Employ techniques like learning rate scheduling, early stopping, and batch normalization to improve model convergence and performance. Regular monitoring of training metrics is essential to avoid issues like overfitting or mode collapse (in GANs).

Deploying Generative AI Solutions

Deployment Strategies

Cloud-Based Platforms: Cloud platforms like Google Cloud AI, AWS SageMaker, and Azure ML offer managed services for deploying AI models, including scalability, monitoring, and integration with other cloud services. These platforms are ideal for organizations that need to deploy models at scale without managing underlying infrastructure.

On-Premise Solutions: For organizations with specific security or compliance requirements, on-premise deployment might be necessary. This involves managing hardware, software, and deployment pipelines internally, often using tools like Docker for containerization and Kubernetes for orchestration.

Performance and Scalability

Containerization: Tools like Docker allow you to package your model and its dependencies into a container, ensuring consistent behavior across different environments. This is crucial for maintaining performance and reliability in production.

Orchestration: Kubernetes can manage containerized applications, providing automated deployment, scaling, and management. This is essential for large-scale deployments where performance and availability are critical.

CI/CD Pipelines: Implementing continuous integration and continuous deployment pipelines ensures that updates to your models are tested and deployed automatically, reducing downtime and ensuring that your model remains up-to-date with the latest data and improvements.

Security Considerations

Encryption: Secure your data and models during both training and deployment by implementing encryption for data at rest and in transit. This is especially important for sensitive applications like healthcare or finance.

Access Controls: Implement strict access controls to ensure that only authorized personnel can interact with your models and data. This includes using tools like IAM (Identity and Access Management) for role-based access control.

Monitoring for Anomalies: Continuously monitor your deployed models for unusual behavior or performance degradation. This could involve setting up alerts for anomalies in prediction patterns or system performance, ensuring that any issues are quickly identified and addressed.

Summary

Selecting the right tools and platforms is a critical step in the success of any generative AI project. By understanding the strengths and capabilities of each framework and platform, you can make informed decisions that align with your project's goals and requirements. Whether you're building from scratch or leveraging pre-trained models, the tools discussed in this chapter provide a solid foundation for creating innovative generative AI solutions.

Key Takeaways

Generative AI Frameworks: TensorFlow, PyTorch, and Keras are the leading frameworks for developing generative AI models, each with unique strengths. TensorFlow is ideal for large-scale production, PyTorch excels in research and experimentation, and Keras offers simplicity for rapid prototyping.

Specialized Libraries: For specific generative AI tasks, such as building GANs, VAEs, or Transformer models, specialized libraries like TensorFlow GAN, PyTorch-GAN, and Hugging Face Transformers provide tailored tools and pre-built models to accelerate development.

Platforms for Training and Deployment: Cloud platforms like Google Cloud AI Platform, AWS SageMaker, and Microsoft Azure ML offer comprehensive services for training, deploying, and scaling AI models. Each platform integrates well with its ecosystem, providing a range of tools and support for different stages of the AI lifecycle.

Comparative Analysis: Selecting the right tool or platform depends on your project's needs. TensorFlow is preferred for production environments, PyTorch is favored for flexibility in research, and newer libraries like JAX are gaining traction for performance optimization.

Pre-trained Models and Transfer Learning: Leveraging pre-trained models can save time and resources. Transfer learning allows you to fine-tune these models for specific tasks, making it an efficient approach when working with limited data.

Building and Training Models: The choice of framework, data quality, and computational resources are crucial factors in the success of training generative AI models. Utilizing GPUs, TPUs, and advanced techniques can significantly enhance model performance.

Deploying AI Solutions: Deployment strategies should consider scalability, security, and performance. Cloud-based platforms provide robust tools for managing deployments, while containerization and CI/CD pipelines ensure reliability and continuous updates.

Chapter 23: Competitors of Generative AI

Introduction

Generative AI stands as a leading technology in creating novel content and data, but it is not alone in the landscape of artificial intelligence. Various competing technologies offer unique capabilities and solutions, each excelling in different areas of AI. This chapter delves into these key competitors, exploring their functionalities, applications, and impacts.

Overview of Competitors

Generative AI faces competition from several other AI technologies, each with its own strengths and limitations. The primary competitors include:

Traditional Machine Learning Models

Overview

Traditional machine learning models, a staple of AI, focus on analyzing existing data to make predictions or classifications. These models use historical data to train and validate their performance, often relying on supervised or unsupervised learning methods. Unlike generative AI, which creates new data, traditional models are designed to interpret and infer from existing datasets.

Key Technologies

Decision Trees: These models use a tree-like graph of decisions to classify data or predict outcomes. They work by splitting the data into subsets based on different attributes, creating a model that makes decisions based on feature values.

Support Vector Machines (SVMs): SVMs are used for classification tasks by finding the hyperplane that best separates different classes in the feature space. They can be linear or nonlinear and are effective in high-dimensional spaces.

k-Nearest Neighbors (k-NN): This algorithm classifies data points based on the majority class of their nearest neighbors in the feature space. It is simple and intuitive, often used for classification and regression.

Naive Bayes: This probabilistic classifier applies Bayes' theorem with strong (naive) independence assumptions between features. It is effective for text classification and other applications where conditional independence is a reasonable approximation.

Applications

- **Medical Diagnostics:** Predictive models analyze patient data to diagnose diseases or predict outcomes, such as predicting cancer progression or patient survival rates.
- **Fraud Detection:** Models are used to identify unusual patterns or anomalies in financial transactions, helping to detect fraudulent activities.
- **Recommendation Systems:** Algorithms suggest products, movies, or content based on user behavior and preferences, leveraging collaborative filtering or content-based methods.

Strengths

- **Well-Established:** These models are extensively researched and applied in various fields, offering robust and reliable performance for many tasks.
- **Predictive Accuracy:** Effective for tasks where historical data is crucial for making informed predictions.
- **Simplicity:** Often easier to interpret and implement, especially for well-defined problems with structured data.

Weaknesses

- **Data Dependence:** Requires large, labeled datasets for training, which can be a limitation in data-scarce scenarios.
- **Limited Creativity:** Focuses on analyzing and interpreting existing data rather than generating new, creative outputs.

Reinforcement Learning (RL)

Overview

Reinforcement Learning (RL) is a branch of machine learning where agents learn to make decisions by interacting with an environment and receiving feedback in the form of rewards or penalties. RL focuses on finding optimal strategies or policies for maximizing cumulative rewards over time.

Key Technologies

Q-Learning: An off-policy algorithm that learns the value of actions taken in different states, aiming to maximize the expected future rewards. It uses a Q-table to store and update action values.

Deep Q-Networks (DQN): Combines Q-learning with deep neural networks to handle complex, high-dimensional state spaces, such as those found in video games or robotic control.

Policy Gradient Methods: These methods directly optimize the policy (a strategy for selecting actions) using gradient ascent techniques. They are useful for environments with large or continuous action spaces.

Proximal Policy Optimization (PPO): An advanced policy gradient method that improves training stability by ensuring that updates to the policy are not too drastic, enhancing learning efficiency and performance.

Applications

- **Robotics:** RL is used to train robots for tasks such as grasping, navigation, and manipulation, allowing them to learn optimal behaviors through trial and error.
- **Game Playing:** RL has achieved remarkable success in playing games like Chess, Go, and complex video games, often surpassing human performance through extensive training.
- **Autonomous Vehicles:** RL helps in developing self-driving cars by learning to navigate complex traffic environments and make driving decisions in real-time.

Strengths

- **Adaptive Learning:** Capable of learning complex behaviors and strategies by interacting with the environment and adjusting based on feedback.
- **Dynamic Environments:** Effective in situations where conditions change over time, requiring adaptive and responsive decision-making.

Weaknesses

- **Training Time:** Often requires significant computational resources and time to train, especially for complex environments with large state and action spaces.
- **Complexity:** Designing reward functions and ensuring stable learning can be challenging, requiring careful tuning and experimentation.

Symbolic AI and Expert Systems

Overview

Symbolic AI, or rule-based AI, focuses on representing knowledge through symbols and logical rules. Expert systems, a subset of symbolic AI, use predefined rules and knowledge bases to solve specific problems by mimicking human expertise.

Key Technologies

Logic Programming: Uses formal logic to represent and reason about knowledge. Languages like Prolog are used to define rules and relationships among symbols.

Rule-Based Systems: Employs if-then rules to infer conclusions or make decisions based on input data. These systems rely on a set of predefined rules and a knowledge base.

Knowledge Representation: Models information using structured formats such as ontologies, semantic networks, and frames to facilitate reasoning and inference.

Applications

- **Medical Diagnosis:** Expert systems diagnose diseases based on symptoms and medical knowledge, providing recommendations for treatment based on established rules.
- **Troubleshooting:** Used in technical domains to identify and resolve issues by following a set of diagnostic rules and procedures.
- **Legal Advice:** Systems offer legal recommendations and insights based on established laws and case precedents, assisting legal professionals and clients.

Strengths

- **Explainability:** Provides clear and interpretable reasoning based on predefined rules, making it easier to understand and trust the system's decisions.
- **Structured Knowledge:** Leverages well-defined knowledge bases and rules, ensuring consistent and reliable problem-solving capabilities.

Weaknesses

- **Scalability:** It can be challenging to scale and adapt to new or unforeseen scenarios, requiring continuous updates to the knowledge base.
- **Knowledge Maintenance:** Demands ongoing maintenance and updates to keep the knowledge base relevant and accurate.

Rule-Based Systems

Overview

Rule-based systems operate based on predefined rules and conditions to make decisions or solve problems. These systems apply a set of rules to input data to derive conclusions or perform actions.

Key Technologies

Production Rules: Rules expressed as if-then statements, where the system applies these rules to data to infer new information or make decisions.

Inference Engines: The component that applies rules to input data, performing logical reasoning to derive conclusions or execute actions.

Knowledge Bases: Stores the rules and factual information used by the inference engine to make decisions and solve problems.

Applications

- **Customer Support:** Automated systems provide responses to customer queries based on predefined rules and frequently asked questions, improving efficiency and consistency.
- **Compliance:** Ensures adherence to regulations and standards by applying rule sets to data, verifying compliance, and identifying violations.

Strengths

- **Simplicity:** Easier to design and implement for well-defined problems with structured rules and conditions.
- **Consistency:** Provides consistent and predictable results based on the given rules, ensuring reliable decision-making.

Weaknesses

- **Limited Flexibility:** Not suited for tasks that require learning from data or adapting to new situations, as the system operates solely based on predefined rules.
- **Maintenance Overhead:** Requires regular updates and maintenance of rules to address new scenarios and changing requirements.

Hybrid AI Approaches

Overview

Hybrid AI approaches integrate multiple AI techniques to combine their strengths and address their individual limitations. These approaches aim to create more versatile and robust systems by leveraging different methods, such as combining neural networks with symbolic reasoning or integrating reinforcement learning with rule-based systems.

Key Technologies

Neuro-Symbolic Systems: Integrates neural networks with symbolic reasoning to combine learning and reasoning capabilities. This approach aims to enhance the interpretability and generalization of AI systems.

Multi-Agent Systems: Utilizes multiple AI agents, each with different capabilities, to collaborate and solve complex problems. These systems can be applied in environments requiring coordination and cooperation among agents.

Integrated Architectures: Combines rule-based systems with machine learning models to enhance decision-making and adaptability. This integration allows for leveraging both structured rules and data-driven insights.

Applications

- **Complex Problem Solving:** Addresses complex problems requiring both learning and reasoning, such as advanced robotics, autonomous systems, and intelligent decision support.
- **Personalized Systems:** Creates personalized recommendations and responses by integrating learning and rule-based approaches, enhancing user experiences and system effectiveness.

Strengths

- **Versatility:** Can address a wide range of tasks by leveraging the strengths of multiple AI methods, providing comprehensive solutions.
- **Enhanced Capabilities:** Combines learning and reasoning to create more powerful and adaptable systems, improving performance and flexibility.

Weaknesses

- **Complexity:** Integrating multiple AI techniques can be complex and require careful design and coordination to ensure seamless operation.
- **Resource Intensive:** This may require substantial computational resources and development effort to implement and maintain effectively.

Human-in-the-Loop Systems

Human-in-the-loop systems incorporate human feedback and expertise into the AI training and decision-making processes.

Active Learning

Overview: Active learning focuses on selecting the most informative data points for labeling, thereby improving model performance with fewer labeled examples.

Competitiveness: This approach complements generative AI by refining models with targeted human feedback, enhancing accuracy and reducing the need for extensive labeled datasets.

Advantages: Efficiently improves model performance and reduces labeling costs by focusing on the most uncertain or valuable data points.

Human-Centered AI

Overview: Human-centered AI emphasizes designing systems that augment human capabilities and facilitate collaboration between humans and AI.

Competitiveness: This approach values human judgment and expertise, making it suitable for applications where human input is crucial, such as creative design and complex decision-making.

Advantages: Enhances the synergy between humans and AI, improving the effectiveness and user satisfaction of AI systems.

Emerging Technologies

Several emerging technologies are making strides in the field of artificial intelligence and could impact or complement generative AI.

Quantum Computing

Overview: Quantum computing uses quantum bits (qubits) to perform computations that classical computers cannot efficiently handle, offering potential breakthroughs in optimization, cryptography, and complex simulations.

Competitiveness: Quantum computing could revolutionize AI by solving problems currently intractable for classical models, potentially impacting generative AI's dominance in certain areas.

Advantages: Provides unprecedented computational power for solving complex problems, potentially transforming various AI applications.

Neuromorphic Computing

Overview: Neuromorphic computing mimics the neural structure and functioning of the human brain, aiming for efficient and adaptive computation.

Competitiveness: Neuromorphic computing could offer energy-efficient processing and real-time learning capabilities, potentially competing with or complementing generative AI in tasks requiring brain-like processing.

Advantages: Provides energy-efficient computation and enhances real-time learning capabilities, supporting applications such as robotics and sensory processing.

Other Notable Technologies

Several other technologies are also noteworthy competitors or complements of generative AI.

Edge AI

Overview: Edge AI involves deploying AI models directly on edge devices, such as smartphones and IoT sensors, to perform computations locally.

Competitiveness: Edge AI is valuable for applications requiring real-time processing and low latency, such as autonomous vehicles and smart home devices.

Advantages: Reduces latency and dependency on cloud infrastructure, enabling real-time decision-making and enhanced privacy.

Bio-Inspired AI

- **Overview**: Bio-inspired AI draws inspiration from biological systems and processes, such as genetic algorithms and neural networks.
- **Competitiveness**: This approach aims to replicate biological intelligence mechanisms, potentially leading to novel AI techniques and applications.
- **Advantages**: Offers innovative problem-solving strategies and insights based on natural intelligence.

Comparative Analysis

Use Cases and Applications

- **Generative AI** excels in creating new data and content, making it ideal for creative applications such as art generation, text creation, and media synthesis.

- **Traditional Machine Learning Models** are well-suited for predictive tasks and classification based on historical data, offering robust solutions for analytics, diagnostics, and recommendation systems.
- **Reinforcement Learning** is effective for dynamic and complex environments requiring adaptive decision-making, such as robotics, game playing, and autonomous systems.
- **Symbolic AI and Expert Systems** provide clear and interpretable reasoning for well-defined problems, including medical diagnostics, troubleshooting, and legal advice.
- **Rule-Based Systems** offer consistent and reliable solutions for tasks with predefined rules, such as customer support and compliance verification.
- **Hybrid AI Approaches** combine multiple techniques to address complex problems, enhancing versatility and capability in applications requiring both learning and reasoning.

Strengths and Limitations

- **Generative AI** is highly creative and versatile but can be resource-intensive and challenging to control.
- **Traditional Machine Learning Models** offer strong performance for predictive tasks but are limited in their creativity and adaptability.
- **Reinforcement Learning** provides adaptive learning but can be slow to train and complex to design.
- **Symbolic AI and Expert Systems** offer explainability and structured knowledge but struggle with scalability and adaptability.
- **Rule-Based Systems** are simple and consistent but lack flexibility and require ongoing maintenance.
- **Hybrid AI Approaches** provide comprehensive solutions but can be complex and resource-intensive.

Choosing the Right Technology

The choice between these technologies depends on the specific use case, desired outcomes, and available resources. Generative AI is ideal for creative tasks, while traditional models and symbolic AI are better suited for structured and predictive tasks. Reinforcement learning is best for dynamic environments, and hybrid approaches offer versatility for complex problems. Each technology has its place in the AI landscape, and the best choice will depend on the unique requirements of the application.

Appendixes

1 - Acronyms

AAE - Adversarial Autoencoder

ABO - Adversarial Bayesian Optimization

ADA - Adaptive Data Augmentation

ADMM - Alternating Direction Method of Multipliers

AEBM - Adversarial Energy-Based Model

ALBERT - A Lite BERT

ATTN - Attention Mechanism (often abbreviated)

B3Net - Balanced Barycenter Networks

BERT - Bidirectional Encoder Representations from Transformers

BIM - Basic Iterative Method (used in adversarial attacks)

BPTT - Backpropagation Through Time

CapsNet - Capsule Network

ChatGPT - Chat Generative Pre-trained Transformer

CLIP - Contrastive Language-Image Pretraining

CLM - Causal Language Model

CNN - Convolutional Neural Network

CEM - Cross-Entropy Method

A Comprehensive Guide

CTC - Connectionist Temporal Classification

CV - Computer Vision

CVAE - Conditional Variational Autoencoder

DAE - Denoising Autoencoder

DCR - Deep Conditional Regression

DCRNN - Diffusion Convolutional Recurrent Neural Network

Diffusion Models - Diffusion Probabilistic Models

DL - Deep Learning

DRL - Deep Reinforcement Learning

DPL - Dual Policy Learning

DQN - Deep Q-Network

DPT - Deep Pyramid Transform

EBM - Energy-Based Model

FastAI - Fast Artificial Intelligence (library)

FSAN - Few-Shot Adversarial Networks

FNN - Feedforward Neural Network

FPN - Feature Pyramid Network

GAT - Graph Attention Network

GAN - Generative Adversarial Network

GANs - Generative Adversarial Networks

GMM - Gaussian Mixture Model

GNN - Graph Neural Network

GPR - Gaussian Process Regression

GRF - Gaussian Random Field

GRU - Gated Recurrent Unit

GSA - Global Self-Attention

GSPN - Generative Structured Prediction Network

HDGAN - High-Definition Generative Adversarial Network

IBP - Interval Bound Propagation

INN - Invertible Neural Network

LSGAN - Least Squares Generative Adversarial Network

LSTM - Long Short-Term Memory

LSUN - Large Scale Scene Understanding Network

MAE - Masked Autoencoder

MCE - Minimum Classification Error

MCL - Monte Carlo Localization

MCMC - Markov Chain Monte Carlo

MFA - Multi-View Factorization

MLP - Multi-Layer Perceptron

MLP-Mixer - Multi-Layer Perceptron Mixer

MIR - Multi-Instance Regression

MMD - Maximum Mean Discrepancy

MSP - Maximum Softmax Probability

NAT - Neural Architecture Transfer

NCE - Noise Contrastive Estimation

NLP - Natural Language Processing

NLG - Natural Language Generation

NVP - Normalizing Flow with Variational Inference

NVDIA - NVIDIA (common in context of GPUs used in training generative models)

OOD - Out-Of-Distribution

PAAE - Probabilistic Adversarial Autoencoder

PBN - Probabilistic Bayesian Network

PGGAN - Progressive Growing GAN

PIL - Python Imaging Library

POMDP - Partially Observable Markov Decision Process

PPO - Proximal Policy Optimization

Q-Learning - Quality Learning

RAE - Regularized Autoencoder

RGP - Reinforced Generative Process

RL - Reinforcement Learning

RLHF - Reinforcement Learning with Human Feedback

SDE - Stochastic Differential Equation

SAM - Segment Anything Model

SNN - Spiking Neural Network

SNR - Signal-to-Noise Ratio

SSL - Self-Supervised Learning

SVAEs - Semi-Supervised Variational Autoencoders

TFA - Transformer with Feature Attention

TD3 - Twin Delayed Deep Deterministic Policy Gradient

TGAN - Temporal Generative Adversarial Network

TTA - Test Time Augmentation

VAE - Variational Autoencoder

VAE-GAN - Variational Autoencoder Generative Adversarial Network

VQ-VAE - Vector Quantized Variational Autoencoder

VQ-VAE-2 - Vector Quantized Variational Autoencoder 2

VGAN - Variational Generative Adversarial Network

WS-GAN - Wasserstein GAN with Spectral Normalization

WGAN - Wasserstein Generative Adversarial Network

WGAN-GP - Wasserstein GAN with Gradient Penalty

XLNet - Extra Long Network

ZSL - Zero-Shot Learning

2 – Frequently Asked Questions (FAQs)

Chapter 01
What is generative AI?

Generative AI refers to systems that create new, original content by learning patterns from existing data. Unlike traditional AI that analyzes data, generative AI generates novel outputs such as text, images, or music, mimicking human creativity.

How does generative AI differ from traditional AI?

Traditional AI focuses on analyzing and making decisions based on existing data, while generative AI creates new content. This means generative AI can produce unique text, images, or other forms of media, extending beyond mere data analysis.

What are some key characteristics of generative AI?

Generative AI is known for its creativity, generalization across various tasks, interactivity with users, and scalability. These features allow it to produce diverse content and adapt to different applications, from art to writing.

What role did neural networks play in the evolution of generative AI?

Neural networks, particularly the perceptron and multi-layer perceptron, marked a shift from rule-based systems to learning-based approaches. These advances laid the foundation for modern generative models by enabling more complex and effective data modeling.

How did Generative Adversarial Networks (GANs) revolutionize the field?

GANs, introduced in 2014, transformed generative AI by using two competing networks—a generator and a discriminator—to create highly realistic outputs. This approach significantly advanced fields like image synthesis and deepfake technology.

What impact have Transformer models had on generative AI?

Transformer models, introduced in 2018, revolutionized natural language processing by allowing models to process entire data sequences simultaneously. This advancement, exemplified by GPT-3, has led to more coherent and contextually relevant text generation.

How is generative AI used in the creative industries?

Generative AI aids in art, music, and writing by producing original content. Tools like DALL-E and GPT-3 help artists and content creators generate unique visuals, compositions, and text, enhancing creativity and productivity.

What are some healthcare applications of generative AI?

In healthcare, generative AI supports drug discovery, enhances medical imaging, and contributes to personalized medicine. It accelerates the development of new treatments and improves diagnostic accuracy by generating synthetic data and models.

What are the main ethical concerns associated with generative AI?

Ethical concerns include bias in training data, potential misuse of deepfakes for misinformation, and issues with content ownership and copyright. Addressing these concerns requires developing fair and responsible AI practices and legal frameworks.

What future trends are expected in generative AI?

Future trends include the development of hybrid models combining different AI architectures, improved efficiency and scalability, and closer integration with human creativity. Ethical AI development and transparency will also be critical as the technology advances.

Chapter 02

What is Deep Learning and how does it differ from traditional machine learning?

Deep Learning is a subset of machine learning that involves neural networks with multiple layers, known as Deep Neural Networks (DNNs). Unlike traditional machine learning, which often relies on feature extraction, Deep Learning automatically learns and models complex patterns from raw data through hierarchical layers of abstraction.

What are the key components of a Neural Network?

Neural Networks consist of neurons, which perform calculations on input data, and layers, including the input layer (receiving raw data), hidden layers (performing intermediate computations), and the output layer (producing final predictions). Training involves adjusting network parameters to minimize prediction errors.

How does Backpropagation work in training Neural Networks?

Backpropagation computes the gradient of the loss function with respect to each weight in the network. This gradient is used to update the weights through optimization algorithms like Stochastic Gradient Descent (SGD) or Adam, aiming to reduce the difference between predicted and actual outputs.

What is the difference between Supervised and Unsupervised Learning?

Supervised Learning involves training models on labeled data, where input-output pairs are provided, focusing on tasks such as classification and regression. Unsupervised Learning involves training models on unlabeled data to find patterns or structures, focusing on tasks like clustering and dimensionality reduction.

Can you explain what Generative Adversarial Networks (GANs) are and their purpose?

GANs consist of two neural networks—the generator and the discriminator—that are trained together in a competitive setting. The generator creates synthetic data, while the discriminator evaluates its authenticity. The goal is to generate realistic data that is indistinguishable from real data.

What is a Variational Autoencoder (VAE) and how does it differ from a GAN?

VAEs encode data into a latent space and then decode it to reconstruct the original data. They focus on learning a probabilistic representation of data. Unlike GANs, which use adversarial training, VAEs learn by maximizing the likelihood of the data and are particularly good at generating diverse samples.

What are Autoregressive Models and where are they commonly used?

Autoregressive Models generate data sequentially, with each element conditioned on previous elements. They are effective for tasks involving sequences, such as text, music, and speech generation. Examples include PixelCNN for images and WaveNet for audio.

How do Transformers contribute to Generative AI and what are their applications?

Transformers use self-attention mechanisms to process data, revolutionizing natural language processing. They are used for generating text, images, and audio by predicting subsequent elements based on prior context. Models like GPT-3 set new benchmarks in text generation and have been adapted for other domains.

What are Diffusion Models and how do they work?

Diffusion Models generate high-quality data by progressively denoising a random signal. They iteratively refine a noisy input to produce detailed and realistic samples, showing promise in tasks such as image generation and data reconstruction.

What are the main applications of Generative Models in AI?

Generative models have diverse applications, including image synthesis (creating realistic images), text generation (producing coherent text), music composition (generating original music), and scientific simulations (modeling complex systems). Each type of generative model contributes uniquely to these applications based on its strengths.

Chapter 03

What are Generative Adversarial Networks (GANs)?

GANs are a class of machine learning frameworks introduced by Ian Goodfellow in 2014, consisting of two neural networks—the generator and the discriminator—that compete in a game to generate realistic synthetic data.

How do GANs work?

GANs work through an adversarial training process where the generator creates synthetic data from random noise, and the discriminator evaluates this data against real data. The generator aims to produce data that the discriminator cannot distinguish from real data, while the discriminator strives to improve its ability to identify fake data.

What are the roles of the generator and discriminator in a GAN?

The generator's role is to create synthetic data that resembles real data. The discriminator's role is to classify data as either real or fake. Both networks are trained iteratively, with the generator improving based on feedback from the discriminator and vice versa.

What is the significance of GANs in artificial intelligence?

GANs have revolutionized data generation by enabling the creation of highly realistic synthetic data. They have significant applications in fields such as computer vision, natural language processing, and creative industries, enhancing capabilities in image and video generation, art, and design.

What are Deep Convolutional GANs (DCGANs)?

DCGANs utilize deep convolutional neural networks for both the generator and discriminator. They are particularly effective in generating high-resolution images by capturing spatial hierarchies and features, making them suitable for tasks like image generation and augmentation.

What is StyleGAN and how is it different from other GANs?

StyleGAN, developed by NVIDIA, introduces a style-based generator architecture that allows for fine-grained control over generated images. It enables manipulation of image attributes such as style and details, making it useful for creating avatars, artistic portraits, and fashion designs.

What is CycleGAN and what problem does it solve?

CycleGAN focuses on unpaired image-to-image translation, allowing images to be transformed from one domain to another without requiring paired examples. It uses cycle-consistency loss to ensure that images can be transformed back to their original domain, making it useful for tasks like style transfer and domain adaptation.

What are some common applications of GANs?

GANs are used in various applications, including realistic image generation, video creation (e.g., deepfakes), art and design, medical imaging enhancement, text-to-image synthesis, and virtual try-on systems in fashion and retail.

How does the training process of GANs work?

GANs are trained in a two-step process: first, the discriminator is updated to improve its ability to classify real and fake data; then, the generator is updated based on the feedback from the discriminator to produce more convincing data. This iterative process continues until the generator creates data that the discriminator can no longer reliably distinguish from real data.

What are the key challenges in training GANs?

Key challenges include achieving stable training, avoiding mode collapse where the generator produces limited variations of data, and ensuring that the discriminator and generator balance each other in terms of performance to prevent one from overpowering the other.

Chapter 04

What are Variational Autoencoders (VAEs)?

Variational Autoencoders (VAEs) are a type of generative model that combines autoencoders with probabilistic graphical models. They learn a probabilistic representation of input data and use this to generate new, coherent data samples. VAEs aim to approximate complex data distributions through Bayesian inference, enabling the creation of diverse and realistic data.

How do VAEs differ from traditional autoencoders?

Traditional autoencoders learn deterministic mappings from input data to a lower-dimensional latent space, limiting their generative capabilities. VAEs extend this concept by learning a probabilistic mapping, where data is encoded into a distribution rather than a fixed point. This allows VAEs to generate more diverse and varied data samples.

What are the main components of a VAE?

The main components of a VAE include:

- **Encoder Network:** Compresses input data into a probabilistic latent space, outputting parameters (mean and variance) of a probability distribution.
- **Latent Space:** A continuous, lower-dimensional representation of data capturing underlying structures and variations.
- **Decoder Network:** Samples from the latent space to reconstruct the original input data, aiming to produce outputs that closely resemble the original data.

What is the role of the latent space in VAEs?

The latent space in VAEs is a compressed, probabilistic representation of the input data. It allows the model to capture and learn the underlying data distribution. This space enables the generation of new data samples by sampling from learned distributions and decoding them back into the data space.

What is the reparameterization trick in VAEs?

The reparameterization trick is a technique used in VAEs to enable gradient-based optimization. It involves expressing the latent variables as a deterministic function of the mean, variance, and a sample from a standard Gaussian distribution. This trick allows backpropagation through the stochastic layers of the model.

What are the key components of the VAE loss function?

The VAE loss function consists of two main parts:

- **Reconstruction Loss:** Measures the difference between the original input and the reconstructed output, ensuring that the decoder produces data similar to the input.

- **KL Divergence Loss:** Regularizes the latent space by ensuring it follows a standard Gaussian distribution, promoting a well-structured latent space and preventing disorganization.

What are some common applications of VAEs in image generation?

VAEs are used in various image generation applications, including:

- **High-Quality Image Synthesis:** Generating realistic images, such as portraits or artwork.
- **Image Editing and Manipulation:** Altering attributes or combining features from different images.
- **Image Super-Resolution:** Enhancing image resolution from low-resolution inputs.

How can VAEs be used for data augmentation?

VAEs generate synthetic data to augment existing training datasets, especially when real data is limited or sensitive. This synthetic data helps improve model performance and generalization by providing additional diverse examples. VAEs can also impute missing or corrupted data by reconstructing it from the latent representation.

What are the benefits of using VAEs for anomaly detection?

VAEs are effective for anomaly detection as they learn the normal data distribution and can identify deviations from this distribution. This ability to detect outliers makes VAEs useful in applications like fraud detection, network security, and quality control.

Can VAEs be used for text and speech generation?

Yes, VAEs can be adapted for text and speech generation. They can generate coherent text sequences for applications like chatbots or creative writing. In speech synthesis, VAEs can create synthetic speech by learning representations of audio signals, useful for text-to-speech systems and voice cloning.

Chapter 05

What are transformer models and why are they important?

Transformer models are a type of neural network architecture introduced in the paper "Attention is All You Need" by Vaswani et al. in 2017. They are important because they use self-attention mechanisms to efficiently handle dependencies between tokens in a sequence, overcoming limitations of previous models like RNNs and CNNs. Transformers have set new standards in natural language processing (NLP) and extended their influence to fields like computer vision and audio processing.

How does the encoder-decoder structure in transformers work?

In the original transformer model, the encoder processes input sequences and converts them into a continuous representation, while the decoder generates output sequences from this representation. The encoder consists of multiple layers with self-attention and feed-forward networks, and the decoder includes additional cross-attention layers that attend to the encoder's output.

What is the role of positional encoding in transformers?

Positional encoding provides information about the position of tokens in a sequence since transformers do not inherently understand token order. By adding positional encodings to input embeddings, transformers can differentiate between tokens based on their position in the sequence, which helps in capturing the sequence's structure and meaning.

What is self-attention and how does it work?

Self-attention is a mechanism that computes attention scores for each token with respect to every other token in the sequence. It creates a weighted representation where tokens are compared and combined based on their relevance. This mechanism allows the model to dynamically focus on different parts of the sequence, capturing complex dependencies between tokens.

How does multi-head attention enhance the self-attention mechanism?

Multi-head attention extends self-attention by running multiple attention mechanisms in parallel, each with different parameters. This approach allows the model to capture various aspects of token relationships simultaneously, improving its ability to understand different contextual meanings and dependencies within the sequence.

What are the key features of GPT models?

GPT (Generative Pre-trained Transformer) models are designed for text generation and understanding. Key features include:

- **GPT-1:** Introduced pre-training on large text data followed by fine-tuning on specific tasks.
- **GPT-2:** Increased model size and training data, demonstrating capabilities in text generation and completion.
- **GPT-3:** Known for its massive scale (175 billion parameters), enabling few-shot learning and broad task performance.
- **GPT-4 and Beyond:** Continued improvements in architecture and training techniques.

How does BERT differ from GPT models?

BERT (Bidirectional Encoder Representations from Transformers) differs from GPT models in its bidirectional approach to context understanding. While GPT models generate text autoregressively, BERT uses bidirectional attention to capture context from both directions in a sequence. BERT is pre-trained using masked language modeling and next sentence prediction tasks, focusing on understanding and representation rather than text generation.

What are some notable variants of BERT and their improvements?

Notable variants of BERT include:

- **RoBERTa:** Refines BERT's training process by removing the next sentence prediction task, increasing training data, and extending training duration.
- **DistilBERT:** A smaller, faster version of BERT that retains much of its performance through knowledge distillation.
- **ALBERT:** Reduces the number of parameters through factorized embedding parameterization and cross-layer parameter sharing.

What is T5 and how does it unify NLP tasks?

T5 (Text-To-Text Transfer Transformer) treats all NLP tasks as text-to-text problems, where both inputs and outputs are text. This unified framework simplifies model training and application across various tasks by framing them consistently as text generation problems.

How does XLNet improve on BERT's bidirectional context?

XLNet addresses the limitations of BERT's bidirectional context by using a permutation-based training objective. This approach captures bidirectional contexts while preserving the autoregressive benefits of previous tokens, leading to improved performance on various NLP tasks compared to BERT.

Chapter 06

What are diffusion models and how do they differ from other generative models?

Diffusion models are a type of generative model that simulates physical diffusion processes to generate data. They work by progressively adding noise to data and then training a model to reverse this noise addition. This process contrasts with other generative models like GANs and VAEs, which use different mechanisms for data generation.

What is the forward diffusion process in diffusion models?

The forward diffusion process involves incrementally adding noise to data over several steps, transforming it into a noisy distribution that approximates pure noise. This process simulates how data becomes increasingly unrecognizable when subjected to noise.

How does the reverse denoising process work in diffusion models?

The reverse denoising process involves training a model to reverse the noise addition from the forward diffusion process. Starting from noisy data, the model iteratively refines it to recover the original data distribution, gradually reconstructing data from random noise.

What role do stochastic differential equations (SDEs) play in diffusion models?

Stochastic differential equations (SDEs) are used to model the dynamics of noise addition during the forward diffusion process. They describe how noise is introduced over time and are central to simulating the diffusion process in diffusion models.

What are the key evaluation metrics for diffusion models?

Key evaluation metrics for diffusion models include Inception Score (IS) and Fréchet Inception Distance (FID). These metrics assess the quality and diversity of generated samples, evaluating their realism and alignment with the intended data distribution.

How do diffusion models generate high-resolution and realistic images?

Diffusion models generate high-resolution and realistic images by iteratively refining noisy data into structured images. They use the reverse denoising process to enhance details and textures, producing high-quality outputs that capture intricate features.

What are conditional diffusion models and how do they differ from standard diffusion models?

Conditional diffusion models generate data based on additional inputs, such as text descriptions or labels. Unlike standard diffusion models, which generate data without specific constraints, conditional models produce samples that adhere to the given conditions or prompts.

Can diffusion models be used for audio generation?

Yes, diffusion models can be used for audio generation. They have demonstrated the ability to produce high-fidelity audio, including speech and music, by simulating the diffusion of noise in audio signals. This approach is useful for synthesizing natural-sounding speech and complex musical compositions.

What is diffusion-based super-resolution and how does it enhance image quality?

Diffusion-based super-resolution involves using diffusion models to enhance the resolution of images. By generating high-resolution details from low-resolution inputs, these models improve image quality and capture finer details through the denoising process.

What are some advanced techniques in diffusion models, and how do they enhance their capabilities?

Advanced techniques in diffusion models include:

- **Conditional Diffusion Models:** Generate data based on additional inputs, allowing for controlled and specific sample generation.
- **Diffusion-Based Super-Resolution:** Enhances image resolution by generating high-resolution details from lower-resolution images. These techniques expand the versatility and applicability of diffusion models, making them useful for a wider range of tasks and improving their performance in various domains.

Chapter 07

What are text generation models, and why are they important?

Text generation models are advanced AI systems that create human-like text based on given inputs. They are important because they enable applications such as content creation, chatbots, and language translation, improving efficiency and creativity in text-related tasks.

What are the key differences between GPT, BERT, and T5?

GPT (Generative Pre-trained Transformer) uses a unidirectional approach to generate text by predicting the next word in a sequence. BERT (Bidirectional Encoder Representations from Transformers) uses a bidirectional approach to understand context from both sides of a word, excelling in comprehension tasks. T5 (Text-to-Text Transfer Transformer) frames all tasks as text-to-text problems, allowing it to handle a wide range of NLP tasks in a unified manner.

How does GPT generate text?

GPT generates text using an autoregressive approach, predicting the next word in a sequence based on the preceding context. This allows it to produce coherent and contextually relevant text across various domains, including creative writing and code generation.

What is the significance of BERT's bidirectional approach?

BERT's bidirectional approach enables it to capture context from both the left and right of a word, providing a deeper understanding of language. This capability enhances its performance in tasks like question answering, sentiment analysis, and named entity recognition.

How does T5 handle different NLP tasks?

T5 handles various NLP tasks by converting them into text-to-text problems. For example, it can generate summaries from long texts or translate text between languages by treating the input and output as text sequences, making it highly versatile.

What are some common applications of text generation models?

Common applications include content creation (e.g., articles and blog posts), creative writing (e.g., poetry and stories), text summarization (e.g., extractive and abstractive summaries), machine translation, sentiment analysis, and conversational AI (e.g., chatbots and virtual assistants).

What are the differences between extractive and abstractive summarization?

Extractive summarization involves selecting key sentences or phrases from the original text to create a summary, while abstractive summarization generates new sentences to convey the main ideas, often rephrasing or rewriting the content for readability and coherence.

What ethical concerns are associated with text generation models?

Ethical concerns include the potential for generating misinformation or fake news, model biases that may lead to discriminatory outputs, privacy issues related to data used for training, and the need for transparency and accountability in how models are developed and deployed.

How can we mitigate the risks of misinformation and bias in text generation models?

Mitigating these risks involves implementing content verification mechanisms, promoting media literacy, using debiasing techniques, ensuring diverse and representative training data, and adhering to ethical guidelines for responsible AI use.

What role do chatbots and conversational AI play in modern applications?

Chatbots and conversational AI systems use text generation models to simulate human conversation, providing automated responses and enhancing user interactions. They are widely used in customer support, personal assistants, and other applications to improve efficiency and user experience.

Chapter 08

What is the main focus of Text Generation?

The role of text generation in natural language processing (NLP) focuses on exploring influential language models like GPT, BERT, and T5, their applications, and the ethical considerations associated with their use.

What are the key language models discussed in this chapter?

The chapter covers GPT (Generative Pre-trained Transformer), BERT (Bidirectional Encoder Representations from Transformers), and T5 (Text-to-Text Transfer Transformer), detailing their architectures, training, capabilities, and applications.

How does GPT differ from BERT in terms of architecture and functionality?

GPT uses a unidirectional transformer architecture to predict the next word in a sequence, while BERT employs a bidirectional approach to capture context from both sides of a word, allowing for a deeper understanding of word relationships.

What are the primary applications of GPT?

GPT is used in content creation, creative writing, code generation, and other areas where generating coherent and contextually relevant text is required, such as writing essays, generating poetry, and assisting in programming tasks.

How does BERT improve tasks like question answering and sentiment analysis?

BERT's bidirectional training allows it to understand context more deeply, which enhances its ability to accurately answer questions and perform sentiment analysis by comprehending nuanced meanings and relationships between words.

What makes T5 unique compared to other language models?

T5 treats all NLP tasks as text-to-text problems, using a unified framework to handle various tasks such as translation, summarization, and question answering, with a transformer encoder-decoder architecture for flexible task adaptation.

How do language models contribute to content creation and creative writing?

Language models like GPT and T5 automate the generation of articles, blog posts, and creative texts, assisting writers by generating coherent content, brainstorming ideas, and exploring different narrative styles.

What are the differences between extractive and abstractive summarization?

Extractive summarization selects key sentences or phrases from a document, while abstractive summarization generates new sentences to convey the core message, with models like BERT excelling at extractive summarization and T5 at abstractive summarization.

What ethical concerns are associated with text generation technologies?

Ethical concerns include the potential for generating misinformation and fake news, inherent biases in language models, privacy issues related to data usage, security risks from malicious text generation, and the need for transparency and accountability.

How can the ethical challenges of text generation be addressed?

To address ethical challenges, strategies include implementing content verification mechanisms, reducing model bias through diverse data and fairness techniques, protecting user privacy, developing security measures, and establishing clear ethical guidelines and transparency practices.

Chapter 09

What is AI music composition, and how does it work?

AI music composition involves using artificial intelligence to create music. AI models learn patterns from existing music data and generate new compositions by analyzing these patterns. Techniques such as Recurrent Neural Networks (RNNs), Transformers, and Variational Autoencoders (VAEs) are commonly used to produce melodies, harmonies, and rhythms.

How do Recurrent Neural Networks (RNNs) contribute to music generation?

RNNs, including Long Short-Term Memory (LSTM) networks, are effective for generating sequences like musical notes and rhythms due to their ability to model temporal dependencies. They excel at composing melodies and harmonies by learning from sequential data.

What role do Transformers play in music composition?

Transformers use attention mechanisms to model long-range dependencies within musical sequences. This allows them to generate complex musical structures by considering different parts of a composition simultaneously, resulting in coherent and intricate musical pieces.

What is music style transfer, and how can AI be used for it?

Music style transfer involves applying the stylistic elements of one piece of music to another while preserving the original content. AI techniques can transfer characteristics such as rhythms, harmonies, and timbres between different musical pieces, allowing for creative transformations and blending of styles.

What are some popular AI tools for music generation?

Popular AI tools for music generation include OpenAI's MuseNet, which creates music across various genres and styles, and AIVA (Artificial Intelligence Virtual Artist), which generates original compositions tailored to specific needs, such as film scores and commercials.

How does WaveNet contribute to audio generation?

WaveNet, developed by DeepMind, is a generative model that produces high-quality audio waveforms using a deep convolutional architecture. It generates audio samples step-by-step, resulting in realistic and natural-sounding speech and music.

What is Tacotron, and how is it used in speech synthesis?

Tacotron is a sequence-to-sequence model for speech synthesis that converts textual input into natural-sounding speech. It combines a sequence-to-sequence framework with a neural vocoder to produce high-quality synthetic speech that mimics human speech patterns.

How does AI enhance dynamic music generation in video games?

AI enhances dynamic music generation in video games by creating adaptive music that changes in response to gameplay events and player actions. This approach provides a more immersive and interactive experience by tailoring the music to in-game conditions.

What are the benefits of using AI in sound design for film and television?

AI in sound design for film and television helps generate realistic or imaginative sound effects and audio textures. This enhances the auditory experience, making it more immersive and engaging by creating tailored soundscapes for specific scenes or themes.

How is AI used for personalized audio content in media and advertising?

AI-generated audio can create personalized content for advertisements and media campaigns by tailoring music and sound effects to target audiences. This personalization enhances the effectiveness of promotional materials and improves audience engagement.

Chapter 10

What are Generative Adversarial Networks (GANs), and how are they used in video synthesis?

GANs are AI models consisting of two neural networks: a generator that creates new video frames and a discriminator that evaluates their realism. GANs are used in video synthesis for tasks like translating video styles, enhancing video resolution, and maintaining temporal consistency across frames.

How does Video-to-Video Translation with GANs work?

Video-to-Video Translation uses GANs to convert videos from one domain to another, such as changing daytime scenes to nighttime or applying artistic styles. This technique involves training GANs to learn domain-specific features and translate them between different visual styles.

What is Video Super-Resolution, and how does it benefit from GANs?

Video Super-Resolution enhances the resolution of low-quality videos by generating high-definition frames. GANs, particularly Enhanced Super-Resolution GAN (ESRGAN), are employed to improve detail and clarity, making videos appear more sharp and realistic.

How do Variational Autoencoders (VAEs) contribute to video generation?

VAEs encode video frames into a latent space and decode them to generate new frames. They are used for frame prediction, which helps in forecasting future video frames, and interpolation, which creates smooth transitions or blending effects between video sequences.

What role does Reinforcement Learning (RL) play in video generation?

RL can be applied to video generation by training agents to make decisions that impact video content. It is used for dynamic scene generation, creating interactive scenes based on user actions, and content personalization, tailoring videos to individual preferences.

What is Neural Radiance Fields (NeRF), and how does it enhance video synthesis?

NeRF is a neural rendering technique that synthesizes novel views of 3D scenes by learning complex lighting and shading effects. It produces photorealistic videos from 3D models, enabling detailed and immersive visual content creation.

How does AI improve visual effects (VFX) in film production?

AI enhances VFX by generating realistic CGI, adding special effects, and creating complex visual elements such as explosions or weather effects. AI techniques streamline the VFX process and increase the realism of visual enhancements in films.

What are some applications of AI in animation?

AI automates parts of animation production, such as generating in-between frames and creating character animations from motion capture data. Additionally, AI-driven style transfer can apply various artistic styles to animations, allowing for creative transformations and aesthetics.

How does AI support immersive content creation in Virtual Reality (VR)?

AI facilitates immersive VR experiences by generating realistic 3D environments and animations. Techniques like neural rendering and video synthesis create dynamic and interactive VR content, enhancing user immersion and engagement.

What are the main challenges facing AI in video and animation generation?

Key challenges include the need for high-quality and diverse training data, substantial computational resources, and ethical concerns related to misinformation and privacy. Addressing these challenges is crucial for advancing AI technologies in a responsible and effective manner.

Chapter 11

How does Generative AI accelerate drug discovery?

Generative AI speeds up drug discovery by designing novel molecular structures and predicting their properties, such as solubility and toxicity. It also enables virtual screening of millions of compounds and simulates drug interactions to identify promising candidates faster.

What is drug repurposing, and how does AI enhance this process?

Drug repurposing involves finding new uses for existing drugs. Generative AI can identify novel applications for these drugs and uncover new drug targets by analyzing large datasets, potentially offering new treatment options for diseases with limited therapies.

How does AI optimize clinical trials?

AI optimizes clinical trials by improving patient selection through precision recruitment, predicting trial outcomes with predictive analytics, and allowing real-time adjustments to trial protocols based on ongoing data. This leads to more effective and efficient trials.

What role does AI play in enhancing medical imaging?

AI enhances medical imaging by applying super-resolution techniques to improve image clarity, reducing noise and artifacts, and using advanced reconstruction methods to obtain high-quality images from limited or suboptimal data.

How does automated image analysis benefit diagnostics?

Automated image analysis benefits diagnostics by providing AI-driven segmentation and localization of regions of interest, extracting features like lesion size and shape, and detecting anomalies and classifying diseases to assist radiologists in making accurate diagnoses.

In what ways does AI improve diagnostic accuracy?

AI improves diagnostic accuracy by integrating imaging data with electronic health records (EHRs) to provide a comprehensive health view and by offering decision support systems that help healthcare professionals interpret complex imaging data and make informed decisions.

How does AI contribute to personalized treatment plans?

AI contributes to personalized treatment plans by analyzing genomic data to identify genetic variants and predict drug responses. It also integrates multi-omics data to understand disease mechanisms and optimize treatment regimens based on individual patient profiles.

What are the benefits of AI-driven personalized drug selection?

AI-driven personalized drug selection offers recommendations for tailored drug regimens based on individual patient data, improving treatment outcomes and minimizing side effects. It also suggests optimal dosages and makes recommendations for behavioral and lifestyle adjustments.

How does AI analyze genomic data for healthcare applications?

AI analyzes genomic data to identify genetic variants associated with diseases, predict how different genetic profiles respond to treatments, and integrate various types of omics data to provide a holistic view of a patient's health, aiding in personalized treatment planning.

What future advancements can we expect from generative AI in healthcare?

Future advancements in generative AI in healthcare are expected to lead to more precise diagnostics, more effective treatments, and enhanced personalized care strategies. Continued developments will likely improve the efficiency of drug discovery, medical imaging, and patient-specific treatment plans.

Chapter 12

What are the main sources of AI bias?

AI bias can arise from historical biases present in training data, sampling bias from unrepresentative data, algorithmic bias due to model design, and feature selection that encodes prejudiced information. These biases can lead to unfair outcomes and reinforce societal inequalities.

How can we address AI bias in generative models?

To address AI bias, it's important to collect diverse and representative data, conduct regular bias audits, implement fairness frameworks, and ensure transparency and accountability in AI decision-making processes.

Who owns AI-generated content?

Ownership of AI-generated content is complex and involves debates over authorship and attribution. Traditional intellectual property (IP) laws may not fully address AI-generated works, leading to discussions about whether IP rights should belong to AI developers, users, or if AI should be recognized as a legal entity.

What are the ethical implications of AI's impact on creativity?

AI's ability to generate content raises concerns about its impact on human creativity, potentially affecting the value and originality of human-created works. Ensuring fair compensation for human creators and considering the balance between AI-generated and human-created content are important ethical considerations.

How does AI affect cultural appropriation and misuse?

AI-generated content that incorporates cultural elements may raise issues of cultural appropriation. Additionally, the misuse of AI-generated works, such as creating deepfakes or deceptive media, poses significant ethical concerns that necessitate safeguards and regulations.

What privacy concerns are associated with AI deployment?

AI deployment often involves extensive data collection and analysis, raising concerns about privacy and surveillance. Protecting personal data, ensuring data security, and implementing robust data protection measures are essential to address these privacy concerns.

How might AI lead to job displacement and economic inequality?

AI's automation capabilities can lead to job displacement and shifts in the labor market. There is also a risk that the benefits of AI may exacerbate economic inequality. Developing policies for workforce transition, reskilling, and equitable access to AI technologies can help mitigate these impacts.

What are the key rewards and opportunities of AI?

AI offers significant rewards such as enhanced efficiency and productivity, innovation and advancement, and improved quality of life through personalization and problem-solving. Leveraging AI for social good can lead to breakthroughs in areas like healthcare, climate change, and disaster response.

What ethical frameworks are needed for AI decision-making?

Ethical decision-making frameworks are essential for addressing moral dilemmas faced by AI systems, particularly in life-critical situations. These frameworks should provide guidelines for responsible AI deployment and accountability mechanisms to ensure ethical outcomes.

How can society balance the risks and rewards of AI?

Balancing the risks and rewards of AI involves addressing ethical and social implications while harnessing AI's potential for positive impact. This includes promoting transparency, implementing fairness frameworks, ensuring equitable access, and fostering innovation to maximize AI's benefits while minimizing negative consequences.

Chapter 13

What are the main challenges in ensuring the accuracy and reliability of generative AI content?

Ensuring accuracy involves using fact-checking algorithms and validation against trusted data sources. Model robustness can be improved by training on diverse datasets and incorporating techniques to handle edge cases and unexpected inputs.

How can generative AI maintain contextual consistency in long-form content?

Techniques like memory networks and attention mechanisms are used to manage long-term dependencies and maintain coherence in long-form content. These methods help ensure that the generated content remains consistent over extended passages.

What are the computational requirements for training and deploying large generative AI models?

Training large models requires significant computational power, including high-performance GPUs or TPUs. Cloud computing solutions can offer scalable training and deployment, while model optimization techniques can help reduce computational and memory demands.

How can we manage the cost of training and operating generative AI models?

Training costs can be managed through careful budgeting for hardware, cloud services, and operational expenses. Operational costs can be mitigated by using cost-effective cloud solutions, optimizing resource usage, and exploring energy-efficient algorithms.

What ethical concerns arise from the misuse of generative AI, such as deepfakes?

The creation of deepfakes and deceptive media raises ethical concerns about misinformation and privacy. Developing detection algorithms, implementing verification systems, and establishing regulations and policies are essential for addressing these issues.

How can we address bias in generative AI models?

Bias detection and mitigation techniques, such as fairness-aware algorithms and diverse training datasets, are important for addressing bias. Inclusive design practices also help ensure that generative models serve diverse populations and avoid discriminatory outcomes.

What are the key considerations for ensuring transparency and accountability in generative AI?

Transparency involves providing insights into the model's decision-making processes, training data, and limitations. Accountability mechanisms, including oversight, audits, and review processes, are essential for ensuring responsible development and deployment.

How can we protect data privacy and security in the context of generative AI?

Data privacy can be safeguarded through techniques like data anonymization and differential privacy. Robust security measures are necessary to protect AI models and data from unauthorized access and potential attacks.

What are the potential impacts of generative AI on employment and labor markets?

Generative AI may lead to job displacement by automating tasks traditionally performed by humans. However, it also creates new opportunities in AI research, content creation, and technology development. Reskilling programs and exploring new career paths can help balance these impacts.

How does generative AI influence media, culture, and public perception?

Generative AI influences media and cultural production by altering how content is created and consumed. Building public trust involves transparent practices and ethical considerations, while engaging with the public and addressing concerns can foster a positive perception of AI technologies.

Chapter 14

How does generative AI enhance predictive analytics in IoT applications?

Generative AI improves predictive analytics by generating synthetic data to simulate various scenarios. This helps in predicting outcomes more accurately, which is valuable for applications in smart cities, agriculture, and industrial operations.

What role does generative AI play in creating real-time data streams for IoT devices?

Generative AI enables IoT devices to generate real-time data streams, which supports dynamic applications like autonomous vehicles and smart grids. This capability allows for continuous monitoring and adaptive responses to changing conditions.

How can generative AI be used to create adaptive user interfaces for IoT devices?

Generative AI can develop adaptive user interfaces by learning from user behavior and preferences. This allows IoT devices, such as smart thermostats, to generate optimal settings and enhance the overall user experience.

What are the key challenges in integrating generative AI with IoT devices?

Key challenges include ensuring data privacy and security, addressing interoperability issues between diverse devices and AI systems, and establishing common standards and protocols for seamless integration.

How does cloud computing support the scalability of generative AI models?

Cloud computing provides elastic compute resources that scale according to the demands of generative AI tasks. This scalability is crucial for handling the intensive processing requirements of training large models and generating high-quality outputs.

What are the benefits of using cloud-based CI/CD pipelines for generative AI models?

Cloud-based CI/CD pipelines facilitate the iterative development and deployment of AI models. They streamline the integration of updates, ensuring that models are continuously improved and deployed efficiently, enhancing performance and reliability.

How does generative AI contribute to drug discovery and development in healthcare?

Generative AI accelerates drug discovery by generating novel molecular structures and predicting their interactions. This integration enhances the efficiency of the drug development pipeline and reduces the time-to-market for new therapies.

In what ways does generative AI influence the creative industries, such as art and design?

Generative AI assists artists and designers by creating novel artwork, patterns, and designs. It also streamlines content production processes in media and entertainment, generating scripts, music, and visual effects for immersive experiences.

How can generative AI be used to advance scientific research?

Generative AI enables virtual simulations and experiments, allowing researchers to explore complex phenomena in virtual environments. It also generates synthetic data to complement real-world datasets, supporting more comprehensive analyses and model training.

What future technologies are likely to impact the integration of generative AI?

Emerging technologies like quantum computing and edge computing are expected to impact generative AI. Quantum computing may enhance AI model training efficiency, while edge computing enables real-time data processing at the network's edge, benefiting applications requiring low latency.

Chapter 15

How does generative AI facilitate artistic collaboration?

Generative AI tools collaborate with artists by providing novel perspectives and techniques, such as unique visual styles and compositions. This collaboration helps artists explore new forms of art and overcome creative blocks.

What is generative design in architecture, and how does AI contribute to it?

Generative design in architecture involves using AI algorithms to analyze architectural data and propose innovative design concepts. AI assists in creating structures that are both aesthetically pleasing and functionally efficient.

How are advanced text generation models transforming creative writing?

Models like GPT-4 enhance creative writing by suggesting plot developments, character traits, and dialogue, helping authors overcome writer's block and explore new storytelling techniques.

What features do AI music generation platforms offer?

AI music generation platforms provide tools for creating melodies, harmonies, and rhythms. These features enable musicians to explore new genres and compositions, expanding their creative possibilities.

In what ways does generative AI contribute to dynamic art installations?

Generative AI enhances interactive art installations by adapting to audience interactions and environmental changes. This creates immersive experiences that evolve in real-time, offering a unique encounter with art.

How does generative AI enable personalized content generation for users?

Generative AI creates detailed user profiles by analyzing behavior and preferences. This allows for highly personalized content, such as tailored news feeds, product recommendations, and targeted marketing.

What role does generative AI play in educational content customization?

Generative AI creates personalized educational materials, such as adaptive quizzes and learning modules, based on student performance and learning styles. This approach improves educational outcomes by catering to individual needs.

How does generative AI enhance virtual worlds in the metaverse?

AI algorithms generate diverse virtual environments, landscapes, and interactive elements in the metaverse. This contributes to a rich and immersive virtual experience, with worlds that evolve dynamically based on user interactions.

What are AI-generated avatars, and how do they improve metaverse experiences?

AI-generated avatars are realistic and customizable digital representations of users in the metaverse. They allow extensive personalization and contribute to more engaging and interactive virtual environments.

What future innovations are expected in generative AI creativity tools?

Future developments in AI creativity platforms are anticipated to include advanced real-time collaboration tools, creative brainstorming features, and automated content generation capabilities, further expanding the possibilities for artists, designers, and content creators.

Chapter 16

What advancements are expected in generative AI model architectures?

Future research will focus on developing next-generation architectures, including advanced transformers and hybrid models combining GANs with VAEs. Innovations like neural architecture search (NAS) will also play a role in discovering high-performing models.

How are researchers working to improve the explainability and interpretability of generative AI models?

Researchers are developing methods to interpret model outputs, such as attention maps and activation visualization. Explainable AI (XAI) techniques are being integrated to provide insights into how models generate content and make predictions.

What are few-shot and zero-shot learning, and why are they important for generative AI?

Few-shot and zero-shot learning techniques aim to enable generative models to perform effectively with limited training data. These methods, including meta-learning and transfer learning, help models generalize from minimal examples, enhancing their performance and flexibility.

How are data augmentation techniques being advanced to improve generative models?

Advanced data augmentation methods, such as synthetic data generation and adversarial training, are being developed to enrich training datasets. These techniques introduce variability and complexity, improving the robustness and generalization of generative models.

What are the current strategies for mitigating biases in generative AI models?

Strategies include implementing fairness constraints, debiasing algorithms, and using diverse training datasets. These approaches aim to ensure that AI systems generate equitable and unbiased outputs.

What role do regulatory frameworks play in the development of generative AI technologies?

Regulatory frameworks are crucial for addressing data privacy, security, and ethical use of AI technologies. Researchers and policymakers are working to establish guidelines that ensure transparency, accountability, and responsible deployment of generative AI systems.

What are some potential breakthroughs in generative AI that we can expect in the near future?

Expected breakthroughs include hyper-realistic content generation (e.g., photorealistic images, high-fidelity audio) and multimodal generative models that integrate and generate content across various data types, enabling richer and more complex interactions.

How might generative AI revolutionize engineering and personalized medicine?

In engineering, generative AI will optimize structures, materials, and systems through generative design algorithms. In personalized medicine, AI will enable tailored treatment plans and drug formulations based on individual genetic profiles, improving healthcare solutions.

What innovations are anticipated in AI-augmented creativity and interactive AI systems?

Innovations will include more sophisticated AI-assisted design tools, creative ideation platforms, and interactive systems that engage in dynamic interactions with users. These advancements will enhance artistic processes and provide more intuitive user experiences.

How is generative AI expected to impact industries such as entertainment, healthcare, and education?

In entertainment, generative AI will create immersive experiences and high-quality content. In healthcare, it will advance research, personalize treatments, and improve diagnostics. In education, AI will offer personalized learning experiences and interactive tools, enhancing education and training effectiveness.

Chapter 17

What is the purpose of building a GAN from scratch in this chapter?

Building a GAN from scratch helps you understand the fundamental components and workings of Generative Adversarial Networks, including the roles of the generator and discriminator, and the adversarial training process.

How do you set up the environment for implementing a GAN?

To set up the environment, you need to install Python along with TensorFlow or PyTorch. You can install TensorFlow with the command pip install tensorflow keras, and ensure you have the necessary libraries for building and training the GAN.

What are the key components of a GAN, and how do they interact?

A GAN consists of two neural networks: the generator, which creates synthetic data, and the discriminator, which evaluates the authenticity of the data. The generator aims to fool the discriminator, while the discriminator works to accurately differentiate between real and fake data.

What is the training process for a GAN, and what are some key considerations?

The training process involves alternating between training the discriminator with real and fake data and training the generator to produce more realistic data. Key considerations include choosing appropriate loss functions, maintaining training stability, and evaluating model performance using metrics like Inception Score or Frechet Inception Distance (FID).

How do you implement a text generator using GPT, and what are the steps involved?

To implement a text generator using GPT, you need to install the Hugging Face Transformers library, load a pre-trained GPT model and tokenizer, and use them to generate text based on input prompts. Experimenting with parameters like temperature and top_k can help control the output's creativity and coherence.

What are some key parameters to adjust when generating text with GPT?

Key parameters include temperature, which controls the randomness of the output, and top_k, which affects the diversity of the generated text. Higher temperatures produce more creative outputs, while lower temperatures yield more conservative results.

How does StyleGAN differ from other generative models, and what are its applications?

StyleGAN is designed for creating high-quality images with intricate style and content control. It allows fine-tuning of various attributes in the generated images, making it suitable for artistic and realistic image creation. Applications include generating realistic portraits, abstract art, and more.

What steps are involved in setting up a StyleGAN project?

To set up a StyleGAN project, you need to install dependencies like StyleGAN2-PyTorch, load a pre-trained model or train your own using a dataset, and then generate images by experimenting with different seeds and parameters.

What are some key considerations for training and using StyleGAN?

Key considerations include using diverse datasets for training, tuning parameters like latent vector dimensions and style weights, and being mindful of the ethical implications, especially regarding copyright and commercial use of generated art.

What are the key takeaways from the hands-on projects in this chapter?

A Comprehensive Guide

The key takeaways include gaining practical experience with generative AI techniques, developing technical skills in model implementation and training, and exploring creative applications of generative AI, from generating realistic images to crafting compelling text.

Chapter 18

What is image synthesis, and how is it used in generative AI?

Image synthesis involves generating new images using AI models, primarily Generative Adversarial Networks (GANs). In generative AI, it creates realistic visuals from scratch, such as human faces or landscapes, with applications in entertainment, product design, and virtual reality.

How does image enhancement with AI differ from traditional methods?

AI-driven image enhancement improves existing images by increasing resolution, reducing noise, and restoring details through deep learning techniques. Unlike traditional methods, which may result in blurry outputs, AI models refine images to achieve clearer and more detailed visuals, useful in fields like medical imaging and photography.

What are deepfakes, and what risks do they pose?

Deepfakes are AI-generated media where a person's likeness is replaced with another's, creating highly realistic but fake content. While they have legitimate uses in entertainment and virtual influencers, they pose risks related to misinformation, privacy invasion, and potential misuse in creating deceptive media.

How can deepfake detection methods help in combating misinformation?

Deepfake detection methods use machine learning models to identify inconsistencies in deepfake media, such as unnatural facial movements or mismatches in audio and video. These techniques are crucial for maintaining media integrity and preventing the spread of misleading content.

What is super-resolution imaging, and where is it most useful?

Super-resolution imaging enhances the resolution of images to provide clearer and more detailed visuals. This technique, using generative AI models, is valuable in remote sensing for environmental monitoring, healthcare for detailed diagnostic images, and consumer electronics for high-definition content.

How does style transfer work, and what are its applications?

Style transfer involves applying the artistic style of one image to the content of another using deep neural networks. This technique blends traditional art with modern photography, with applications in graphic design, creating personalized social media filters, and artistic projects.

What role does AI play in artistic creation beyond style transfer?

AI contributes to artistic creation by generating original visual and musical compositions. Artists use AI to explore new creative possibilities, producing novel artworks and music compositions that push traditional art boundaries, with some AI-generated pieces gaining recognition in art exhibitions.

How does generative AI contribute to 3D model generation?

Generative AI models can create detailed 3D models from 2D images or textual descriptions. This technology revolutionizes fields like gaming and architecture by rapidly generating complex 3D environments and structures, significantly reducing manual modeling efforts.

What are some industrial applications of generative AI in 3D modeling?

In industries such as automotive design and robotics, generative AI is used to create and test 3D models before physical production. This accelerates the design process, allows for innovative design testing, and ensures components function as intended through virtual simulations.

What ethical considerations arise with the use of generative AI in computer vision?

Ethical considerations include the potential misuse of deepfakes for misinformation, privacy concerns with synthetic media, and the impact of AI-generated art on traditional creativity and intellectual property. As generative AI technology evolves, addressing these ethical challenges is crucial for responsible and beneficial use.

Chapter 19

What is text generation in the context of generative AI?

Text generation involves creating new, coherent, and contextually relevant text using AI models like GPT-4. These models generate content based on input data, enabling applications in creative writing, automated content creation, and personalized recommendations.

How does text summarization work with generative AI?

Text summarization uses AI to condense longer texts into shorter summaries while preserving key information. Techniques include extractive summarization, which extracts important sentences, and abstractive summarization, which generates new sentences to convey the core message.

What are conversational agents, and how do they utilize generative AI?

Conversational agents, powered by generative AI, simulate human conversation. They use natural language understanding to interpret user inputs and dialogue management to maintain coherent interactions. Applications include customer support, personal assistants, and therapeutic conversations.

What is the difference between rule-based and AI-powered chatbots?

Rule-based chatbots follow predefined scripts and respond to specific keywords, making them suitable for simple tasks. AI-powered chatbots use machine learning to understand and respond to a wider range of inputs, offering more flexible and sophisticated interactions.

How has machine translation improved with generative AI?

Generative AI has advanced machine translation through neural machine translation (NMT), which uses neural networks to understand context and provide more accurate translations. This includes real-time translation capabilities and applications in online translation services and multilingual support.

In what ways can generative AI enhance content creation and copywriting?

Generative AI assists in content creation by suggesting topics, generating drafts, and optimizing text for readability and SEO. In copywriting, AI helps create compelling headlines, persuasive marketing copy, and personalized messages for various audience segments.

What is sentiment analysis, and how does AI improve it?

Sentiment analysis classifies text into categories like positive, negative, or neutral. Generative AI improves accuracy by understanding contextual nuances and can be applied to customer feedback, social media monitoring, and brand sentiment analysis.

How does emotion analysis differ from sentiment analysis?

Emotion analysis identifies specific emotions expressed in text, such as joy or sadness, providing deeper insights than general sentiment analysis. This is useful for market research and crisis management, helping businesses understand emotional responses and address concerns effectively.

What role do transformers play in generative AI for NLP?

Transformers, like GPT-4, are crucial for generative AI in NLP. They leverage large-scale datasets and deep learning to generate high-quality, contextually relevant text, setting new standards in text generation and summarization.

What are some practical applications of generative AI in conversational agents and chatbots?

Practical applications include enhancing customer support by handling routine queries, providing personalized assistance through virtual assistants, and offering therapeutic support in mental health. AI-driven conversational agents improve interaction quality and efficiency across various domains.

Chapter 20

What is generative AI, and how does it impact art and creativity?

A Comprehensive Guide

Generative AI refers to artificial intelligence systems that can create new content, such as images, music, and text, by learning from existing data. In art and creativity it impacts these fields by providing tools that assist artists and creators in generating novel works, enhancing production processes, and exploring new artistic possibilities.

How does AI-generated music work?

AI-generated music uses deep learning algorithms to analyze vast amounts of music data, learning patterns, structures, and styles to create original compositions. Technologies like Recurrent Neural Networks (RNNs), Generative Adversarial Networks (GANs), and Variational Autoencoders (VAEs) enable AI to generate melodies, rhythms, and entire pieces in various genres.

What are some key technologies used in AI-generated art?

Key technologies in AI-generated art include Generative Adversarial Networks (GANs), which create high-quality images by learning from existing artwork; Neural Style Transfer, which combines the content of one image with the artistic style of another; and DeepDream, which enhances and modifies images using convolutional neural networks.

How is generative AI used in film production?

Generative AI enhances film production through automated scriptwriting, visual effects (VFX), and character creation. AI tools can generate dialogue, create realistic visual effects, and produce virtual actors or digital doubles, simplifying complex post-production processes and enabling new creative possibilities.

What role does AI play in animation?

In animation, AI facilitates tasks like character animation, storyboarding, and style adaptation. AI tools can automate frame generation, create dynamic storyboards, and apply various artistic styles to animations, improving efficiency and expanding visual experiences.

How is generative AI applied in architecture and fashion design?

In architecture, generative AI is used to explore diverse design options, optimize structural elements, and assist in smart city planning. In fashion, AI helps design clothing, predict trends, and provide personalized recommendations through trend analysis and virtual try-ons.

Can AI support creative writing, and if so, how?

Yes, AI supports creative writing by assisting with plot development, dialogue generation, and editing. AI tools use Natural Language Processing (NLP) and machine learning to analyze literature, generate narrative elements, and provide feedback on writing style, grammar, and coherence.

What are some notable case studies of AI in art and creativity?

Notable case studies include:

- Refik Anadol's use of AI for immersive, data-driven art installations.
- The Obvious Art Collective's AI-generated portrait "Edmond de Belamy," which sold at auction.
- Taryn Southern's collaboration with Amper Music to create the album "I AM AI."

What are the ethical considerations when using generative AI in creative fields?

Ethical considerations include ensuring the originality of AI-generated content, addressing potential biases in AI models, and respecting intellectual property rights. It's important to develop and adhere to ethical guidelines to manage these challenges responsibly.

How is generative AI expected to evolve in the future of art and creativity?

Generative AI is expected to continue evolving, offering even more advanced tools and techniques for artists and creators. Future developments may include more sophisticated AI models, greater integration of AI in creative processes, and new forms of artistic expression that push the boundaries of traditional practices.

Chapter 21

What is the role of DALL-E in art and entertainment, and how has it been used in real-world applications?

DALL-E, developed by OpenAI, generates images from textual descriptions, enabling users to visualize concepts that may not exist in reality. It is used in advertising agencies to rapidly prototype visual content for marketing campaigns, offering multiple design options quickly and creatively.

How has generative AI contributed to drug discovery, and what is an example of its impact?

Generative AI models, especially GANs, have accelerated drug discovery by generating novel molecular structures. For instance, Insilico Medicine used GANs to discover new molecules for cancer treatment, significantly advancing several drug candidates to preclinical testing stages.

How does GPT-3 enhance content creation, and what are some practical applications?

GPT-3 is a state-of-the-art text generation model that produces coherent, contextually relevant text. It is used in platforms like Copy.ai to assist in generating marketing content, blog posts, and other text-based content, enhancing productivity and automating content creation.

What is deepfake technology, and how was it utilized in the film industry?

Deepfake technology, powered by GANs, creates highly realistic synthetic media, including images and videos. In "The Irishman," deepfake technology was used to de-age actors, enabling them to portray characters over several decades and enhancing visual storytelling.

How are generative models used in finance, and what benefits do they provide?

Generative models are used in finance to simulate market conditions and develop trading strategies. For example, Goldman Sachs uses these models to forecast market trends and test trading algorithms, improving their ability to anticipate market changes and refine strategies.

How does generative AI support personalized learning in education?

Generative AI creates customized learning experiences by analyzing students' progress and preferences. For example, Khan Academy uses generative AI to generate personalized exercises and learning paths, enhancing student engagement and learning outcomes.

What role does generative AI play in product design and customization within retail?

Generative AI assists in designing new products and personalizing customer experiences. Nike's "Nike By You" platform uses generative AI to offer personalized shoe designs, allowing customers to create products tailored to their preferences and enhancing their shopping experience.

What are the key lessons learned from successful generative AI projects regarding data quality?

High-quality and diverse datasets are crucial for training effective generative models. Successful projects emphasize the importance of investing in comprehensive data collection and curation to improve model performance and output quality.

What ethical considerations should be addressed when deploying generative AI, and how can they be managed?

Ethical challenges such as bias and privacy must be addressed in generative AI projects. Implementing ethical guidelines and mechanisms to ensure responsible use of technology helps address potential issues and ensures fair and responsible deployment.

Why is continuous improvement important in generative AI projects, and what approach is recommended?

Continuous improvement is essential for enhancing model performance and applicability. Adopting an iterative approach, where models are regularly updated based on user feedback and performance metrics, leads to better results and increased effectiveness.

Chapter 22

What are the primary generative AI frameworks, and how do they differ?

The primary frameworks are TensorFlow, PyTorch, and Keras. TensorFlow is known for its scalability and integration with Google tools, making it ideal for production environments. PyTorch is favored for its dynamic computation graph, which enhances flexibility and is popular in research. Keras, which runs on top of TensorFlow, Theano, or CNTK, is designed for ease of use and rapid prototyping.

How does TensorFlow support generative AI tasks?

TensorFlow supports generative AI through tools like TensorFlow GAN (TF-GAN) for Generative Adversarial Networks (GANs) and TensorFlow Probability for probabilistic models, including Variational Autoencoders (VAEs). These tools enable users to build, train, and deploy generative models efficiently.

What makes PyTorch a preferred choice for research-oriented projects?

PyTorch is preferred for its dynamic computation graph, which allows for more intuitive model building and debugging. This flexibility, combined with its integration with the Python ecosystem, makes PyTorch particularly suitable for experimentation and research.

What are Hugging Face Transformers, and why are they significant?

Hugging Face Transformers is a library that provides access to a vast repository of pre-trained models for natural language processing (NLP) tasks, such as text generation. The library is significant because it simplifies the use of state-of-the-art models like GPT-3, BERT, and T5, making advanced NLP tasks more accessible.

What are the benefits of using pre-trained models in generative AI?

Pre-trained models offer several benefits, including reduced development time and computational resources. They provide a strong starting point by leveraging models trained on large datasets, which can be fine-tuned for specific tasks, such as text generation or image synthesis.

How does AWS SageMaker facilitate the training and deployment of generative AI models?

AWS SageMaker provides a fully managed environment for building, training, and deploying machine learning models. It supports various frameworks, offers pre-built algorithms for generative tasks, and provides endpoints for real-time inference. SageMaker's scalability and integration with other AWS services enhance its capabilities for managing AI models.

What role does Azure Machine Learning play in the development of generative AI models?

Azure Machine Learning is a cloud-based service that supports building, training, and deploying machine learning models. It offers automated machine learning (AutoML) for rapid development and tools for model monitoring and deployment. Its integration with other Azure services and high-performance computing capabilities make it a robust choice for AI projects.

What are the advantages of using JAX for high-performance computing in generative AI?

JAX combines NumPy's API with automatic differentiation, making it highly effective for tasks that require fast execution and parallelization. It is particularly useful for high-performance computing applications, such as gradient-based optimization in large-scale models.

What are the key considerations for deploying generative AI models?

Key considerations include choosing between cloud-based platforms or on-premise solutions, ensuring scalability and performance, and implementing security measures. Cloud platforms offer managed services and scalability, while on-premise solutions may be necessary for specific security needs. Containerization, orchestration with Kubernetes, and CI/CD pipelines are important for deployment management.

How can transfer learning enhances the development of generative AI models?

Transfer learning allows developers to adapt pre-trained models to new, related tasks. This approach reduces the amount of training data needed and accelerates the development process. By leveraging knowledge from related domains, transfer learning can improve performance and efficiency, particularly when labeled data is limited.

Chapter 23

What distinguishes traditional machine learning models from generative AI?

Traditional machine learning models analyze and interpret existing data to make predictions or classifications. They rely on historical data and established methods such as decision trees, SVMs, and k-NN. In contrast, generative AI creates new content and data, focusing on generating novel outputs rather than analyzing existing ones.

How does reinforcement learning (RL) compare to generative AI in terms of applications?

RL is focused on learning optimal decision-making strategies through interactions with an environment and feedback. It's particularly effective in dynamic scenarios like robotics and game playing. Generative AI, on the other hand, excels in creating new content and data, such as text, images, and music.

What are the main advantages and disadvantages of symbolic AI and expert systems compared to generative AI?

Symbolic AI and expert systems use predefined rules and logical reasoning, providing clear and interpretable results. They are useful for structured tasks like medical diagnosis and troubleshooting. However, they can struggle with scalability and adapting to new scenarios. Generative AI, while versatile and creative, can be resource-intensive and challenging to control.

In what scenarios would rule-based systems be preferred over generative AI?

Rule-based systems are ideal for tasks with well-defined rules and structured data, such as customer support and compliance verification. They offer consistency and simplicity but lack the flexibility and creativity of generative AI, which is better suited for dynamic and creative tasks.

What are the benefits of hybrid AI approaches compared to using generative AI alone?

Hybrid AI approaches combine multiple techniques, such as neural networks and symbolic reasoning, to leverage the strengths of each method. This can create more versatile and robust systems for complex problems. Generative AI alone may lack the adaptability and comprehensive problem-solving capabilities that hybrid approaches offer.

How do human-in-the-loop systems enhance the performance of AI compared to generative AI?

Human-in-the-loop systems incorporate human feedback and expertise into AI training, improving model performance and reducing the need for extensive labeled datasets. This can refine models and enhance their accuracy, which complements generative AI's creative capabilities by ensuring models are more aligned with human judgment.

What role do emerging technologies like quantum computing and neuromorphic computing play in the AI landscape?

Quantum computing offers unprecedented computational power for solving complex problems and could impact generative AI by handling tasks currently intractable for classical models. Neuromorphic computing mimics brain-like processing, providing energy-efficient computation and real-time learning capabilities, potentially complementing or competing with generative AI in certain applications.

How does edge AI differ from generative AI in terms of deployment and performance?

Edge AI involves deploying AI models directly on edge devices for real-time processing with low latency, which is beneficial for applications like autonomous vehicles and smart devices. Generative AI often relies on cloud infrastructure for intensive computation and data generation, whereas edge AI focuses on immediate, localized decision-making and enhanced privacy.

What are the key limitations of traditional machine learning models when compared to generative AI?

Traditional machine learning models are limited by their reliance on historical data and their lack of creativity. They excel in predictive tasks but cannot generate new, creative content. Generative AI, on the other hand, is designed for creating novel data and outputs, which is beyond the scope of traditional models.

When might a business choose to use symbolic AI or expert systems over generative AI?

A business might choose symbolic AI or expert systems when the task requires clear, interpretable reasoning based on predefined rules, such as legal advice or troubleshooting technical issues. These systems provide consistent and understandable results, which can be crucial for applications where transparency and reliability are prioritized over creativity.

www.ingramcontent.com/pod-product-compliance
Lightning Source LLC
Chambersburg PA
CBHW052143220526
45471CB00004B/1508